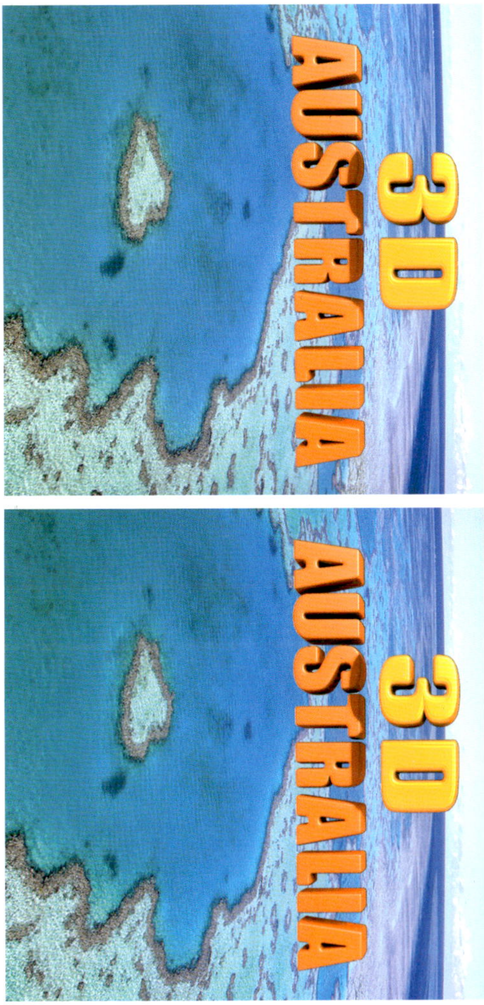
3D
AUSTRALIA
3D
AUSTRALIA

ACKNOWLEDGMENTS

What fun it is to make beautiful books! But we didn't do it alone and we would like to extend our special thanks to the companies and individuals who have supported us on this exciting new project.

To **Qantas** – the best airline in the world – you really epitomise the Australian Spirit and we value your support.

To **Nikon** – we admire your pioneering spirit that helped us create our specialised 3-D digital camera rigs.

To **Apple Computers** – congratulations on producing innovative computers that are designed for creative people.

To Peter Moxom of **Discreet** – we appreciate your generosity in providing our 3-D title page graphics.

To our families – our greatest earthly treasures are our wives and children and we thank you all for the sacrifices you made during the making of this book.

To the 3-D enthusiasts – Ray and Nancy Moxom, Brian Beatty, Franz Miller, Allan Griffin, David Stuckey, Mark Blum and Robin Ford who have willingly given great support and valuable advice on this project.

To our fantastic production and distribution team – hats off once again to Janet Gough, Gary Allen and Kristy Allen, publicist Elizabeth Heusler and writer Dallas Sherringham.

You have all helped to make our dream a reality. Thank you one and all and may you be blessed for the seed you have sown.

Leo Meier and Ken Duncan

INTRODUCTION

Throughout my life there have been many special signposts that have guided my passion for capturing the beauty of God's creation through photography.

As a child I marvelled at the photos my father had taken of some of Australia's last indigenous tribes as a young missionary with his Kodak Bellows camera. When I was sixteen I watched, entranced, as my first black and white photo appeared as a print in the developer tray at a photography camp. At 27 years of age I discovered panoramic photography and to this day I love that particular format.

In early 1993, I wandered into a second-hand camera store looking for treasures. There I found an old 3-D viewer complete with a set of historic images in black and white stereo pairs and was totally captivated. Looking at those amazing three-dimensional images was like being transported back through time to participate in history. Right there and then I bought my first 3-D camera and viewer and couldn't wait to try my hand at this wonderful way of capturing moments frozen in time.

Over the years since the purchase of that first 3-D camera I have firmly believed that there must be a way to revive this awesome method of viewing images so that the general public can once again share the experience.

This book is the first time that a 3-D book has covered all of Australia and hopefully it will be the first of many. It is brought to you with great respect for all the 3-D photographers who have preceded us and I would like to acknowledge the help of our many 3-D friends who are still passionate about this fantastic way of seeing the world.

I hope you enjoy the adventure, as it really is the next best thing to actually being there.

Enjoy the Journey

Ken Duncan

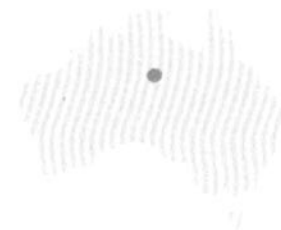

GOD'S MARBLES, WAUCHOPE, NT

The stunning Devil's Marbles in Central Australia should be called God's Marbles because they are such a unique creation. Located 106 kilometres south of Tennant Creek alongside the Stuart Highway, these large spherical boulders were formed by the weathering of granite outcrops on the wide quartz plain. They are particularly stunning when they come aglow with the golden yellow and deep red hues of the setting sun, and cast shadows way out across the desert. The area is now a conservation reserve. To the east is the remote Davenport Range National Park. Virtually every visitor to this amazing formation has a photo of themselves standing amongst the marbles.

Photograph by Leo Meier

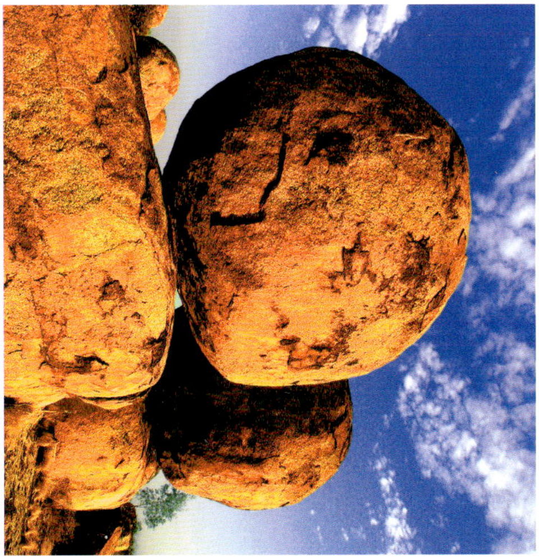
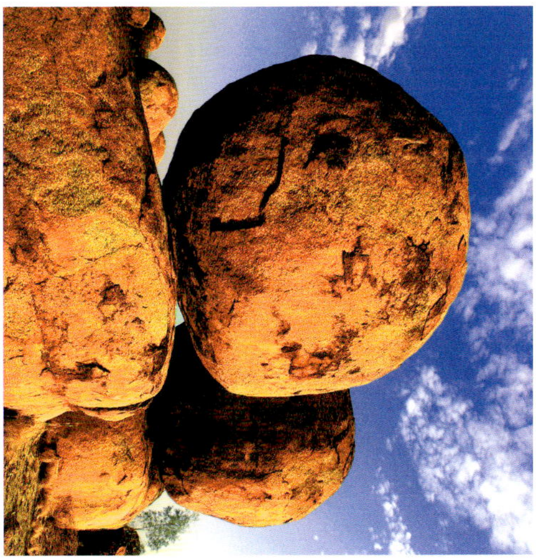

HILL INLET, WHITSUNDAY ISLAND, QLD

Magnificent Hill Inlet in the Whitsundays is Australia's tropics at its best. This view shows the amazing turquoise waters of the Coral Sea blending with the pure white silica sands of the island. A lone yacht enjoys the stunning setting.

While such places are isolated from mainland Australia, they are within easy reach of popular tourist destinations such as modern Hamilton Island. Simply climb into a tour boat or yacht at Hamilton Island Marina and you are soon on your way to paradise – turn right at the headland and go straight ahead for the day of your life.

The tall mountains of the islands – their headlands crowned by giant Norfolk pines – offer a perfect vertical contrast to the quiet blue waters. At every new turn, as you pass between the islands, new vistas open up before you, each one more stunning than the last. No mortal gardener could ever hope to create a scene so complete in its symmetry and humbling grandeur.

Photograph by Ken Duncan

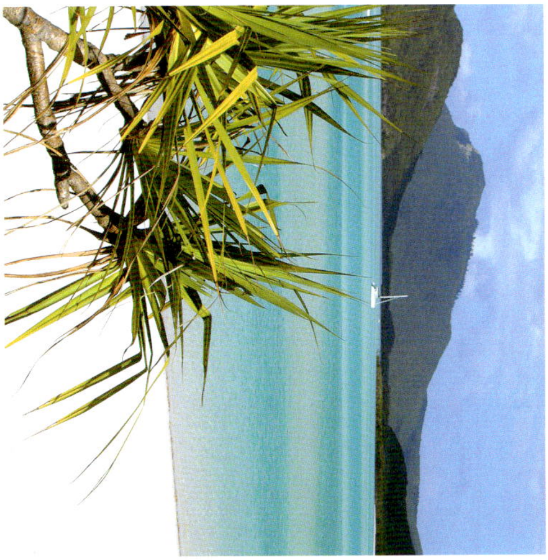

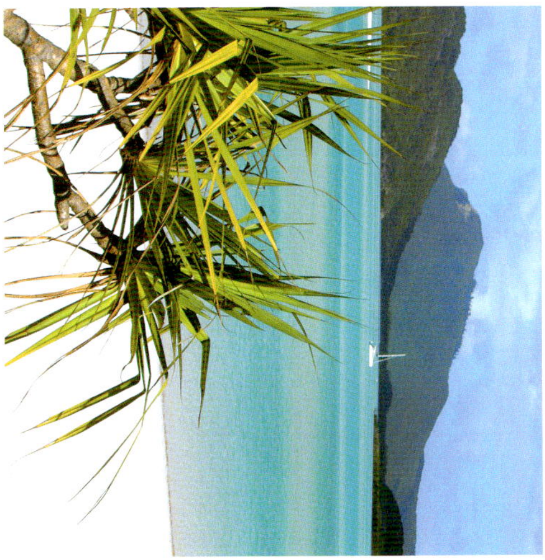

PINNACLES, NAMBUNG NATIONAL PARK, WA

The strange world of The Pinnacles north of Perth has long baffled and entranced visitors to this part of Western Australia. You'd be forgiven if you thought it was a long lost sculpture park of a forest suddenly turned to stone.

Over a large area, beautifully sculpted formations rise from the plain and in the late afternoon sun they glow and throw mysterious shadows. It is a display no mortal could ever hope to achieve.

Scientists say these thousands of limestone pillars are all that remains of a thick bed of limestone throughout the area. It is now known as Nambung National Park and nearby are beautiful beaches with unspoiled waters ideal for a relaxing break.

Photograph by Ken Duncan

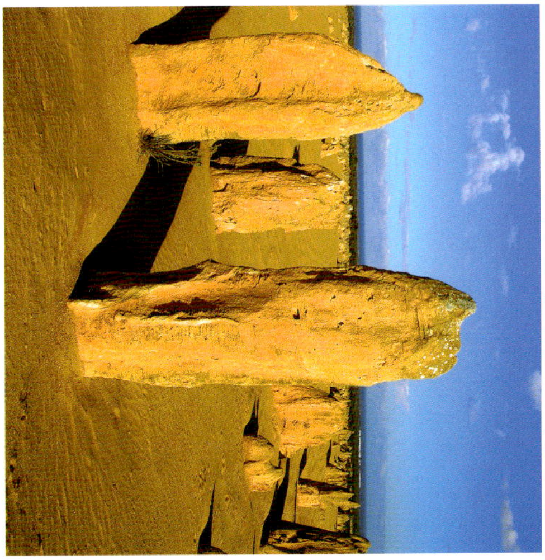

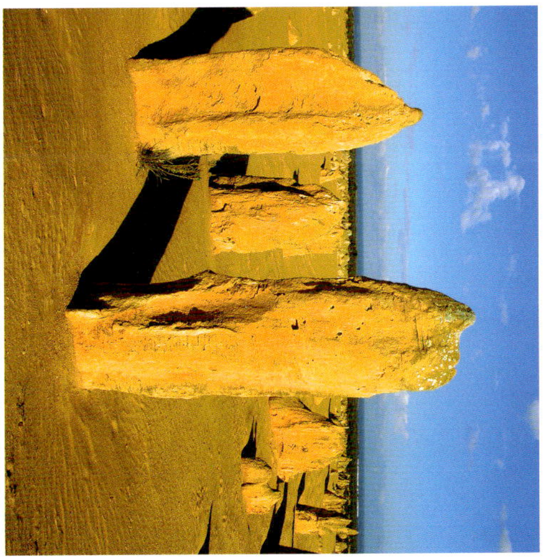

WHITE POINTER SHARK, SA

Imagine the danger involved in capturing a shot as dramatic as this. The photographer is poised at the side of the boat, knowing that somewhere out there lurks Jaws, the most feared creature of the deep. Suddenly the ocean erupts in a volcano of exploding water and muscle, as the giant White Pointer Shark leaps towards him. Half its length is out of the water as it snaps and thrashes about – his best hope is to take the shot and get out of there!

White pointers are mostly active in cool waters where fewer people enter the ocean, but such is its size and power, it accounts for more than a third of the fatalities where the species can be identified. The great white shark is warm-blooded and has more efficient muscles than most shark species, giving it greater speed and power. Most specimens grow to around 5 metres in length and roam widely seeking their favourite prey, which includes large fish, seals and even sea birds

Photograph by Mark Blum

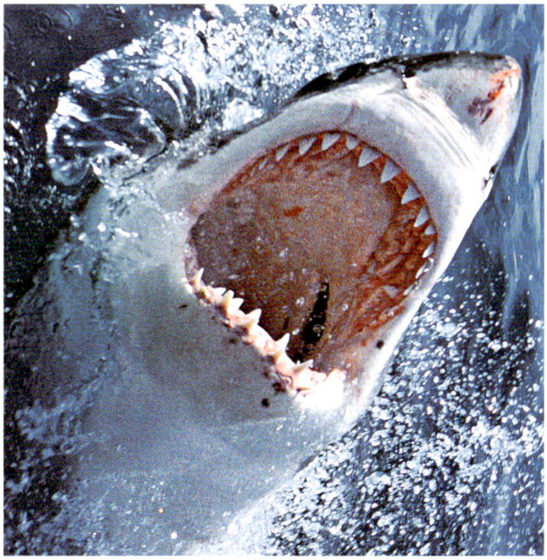

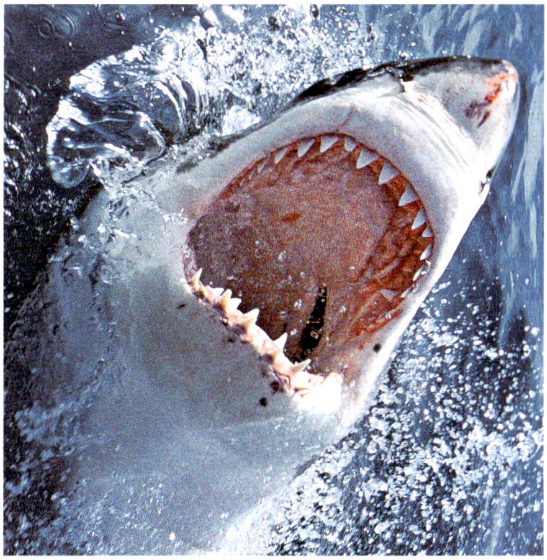

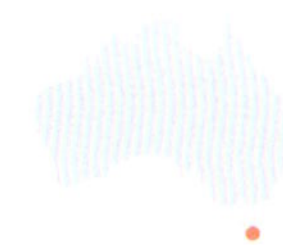

RUSSELL FALLS, MT FIELD NATIONAL PARK, TAS

Multi-tiered Russell Falls, located in Mount Field National Park, is a popular spot for visitors. This is an amazing place with constant moisture in the air giving it the feel of a tropical glasshouse. The splash of water cascading on the rocks is soothing to the senses and you need to sit for a while and take it all in. The falls plunge in two 40-metre stages over rock ledges, with clumps of vegetation separating the various drops and adding to the primeval atmosphere.

Mt Field, Tasmania's oldest national park, is located 80 kilometres north-west of Hobart and is easily accessible for most visitors, even featuring wheelchair access. The surrounding forest has trees more than 200 years old and huge tree ferns, with mosses and lichens clinging to every boulder and log. Trails in the area allow access to moorland, lakes, forest and wide mountain views. There is also a waterfall circuit that takes in Russell, Horseshoe and Lady Barron Falls.

Photograph by Ken Duncan

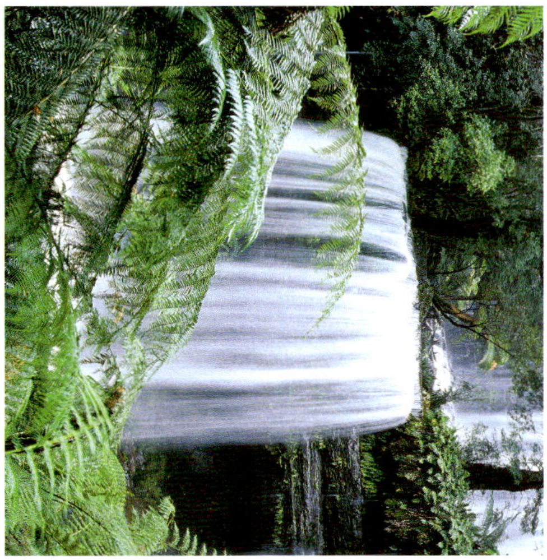

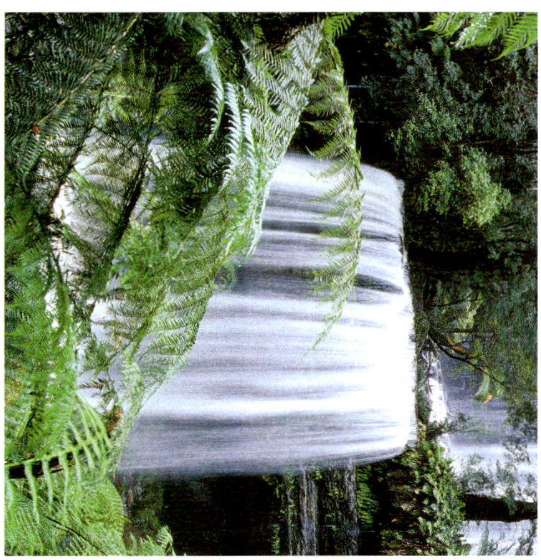

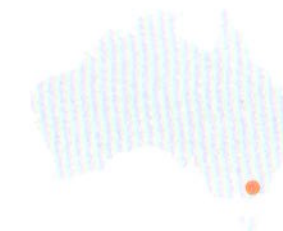

WALLACE HUT, FALLS CREEK, VIC

The magical late afternoon light spreads its golden glow over historic Wallace Hut near Falls Creek. Gnarled snow gums, twisted into fantastic shapes by the harsh conditions of winter, surround this refuge high in the Victorian Alps.

Built in 1898 from snow gum slabs and woollybutt shingles, this timeworn cattleman's hut is thought to be the oldest on the high plains. It is one of more than 100 huts in the Bogong area of the Alpine National Park.

Australia is not generally known for its alpine mountains, but this region perfectly illustrates the wild ranges that dominate the landscape south of Canberra on the NSW-Victoria border. It is the land of legendary cattlemen and the home of *The Man From Snowy River*.

Photograph by Ken Duncan

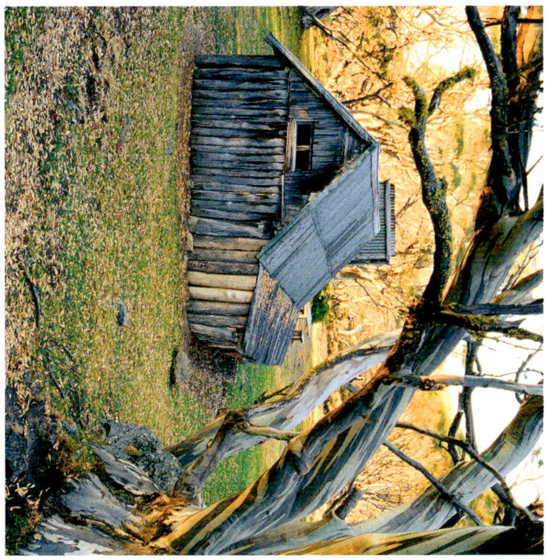

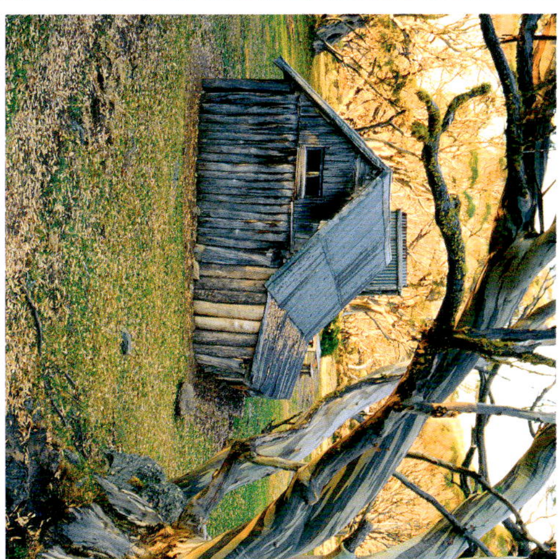

SURF LIFESAVERS, SYDNEY, NSW

Australia's surf lifesavers are the guardians of our nation's beaches. Many of these big-hearted people who take up the call of service and enjoy being part of an esteemed history, are everyday heroes who are continually saving lives. They can spend their weekends rescuing people from treacherous seas then, on Monday morning, return to work or school as if nothing had happened.

During surf carnivals they come together to test their skills against the best in the land and one of the most exciting events, fraught with danger, is surfboat racing. Bashing and crashing through big seas, the boats have to dodge each other while trying to master the ever-changing currents and sandbanks.

Photograph by Allan Griffin

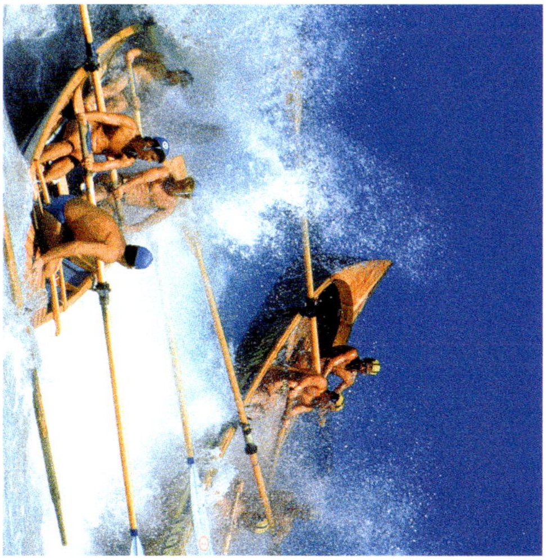

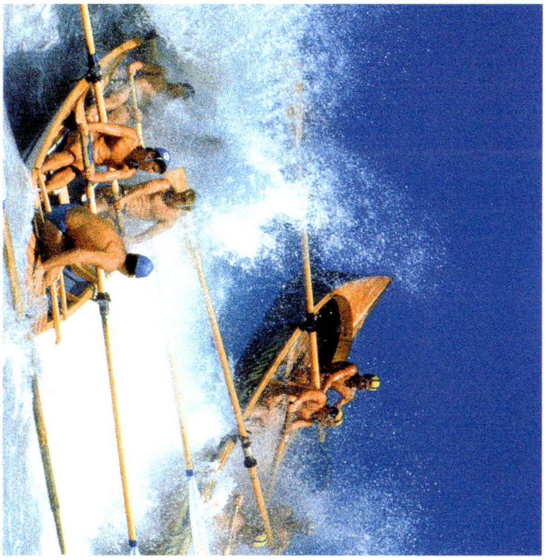

KATA TJUṮA SUNSET, NT

Look to the west of Uluru and you'll see an intriguing rock formation glowing in the distance that immediately demands your attention. You first notice Kata Tjuta (also known as The Olgas) as a cluster of faraway mountaintops when visiting Uluru. As you travel closer, the sheer majesty of this place draws you in. If Uluru has the look and feel of a living thing, Kata Tjuta looks like the most ancient place on earth. It is as if nature built her own version of the pyramids and left them there for all to enjoy. Aboriginal legends tell of a race of giants who sank into the sand, hence the name Kata Tjuta, or "many heads". At sunset the haunting domes of Kata Tjuta take on a special magic. Names such as *Valley of the Winds* have a touch of Egypt about them and they soon set your imagination racing. This wild but deceptively alive landscape is the home of euros and other marsupial species that thrive in the deep gaps between the rock mountains.

Photograph by Leo Meier

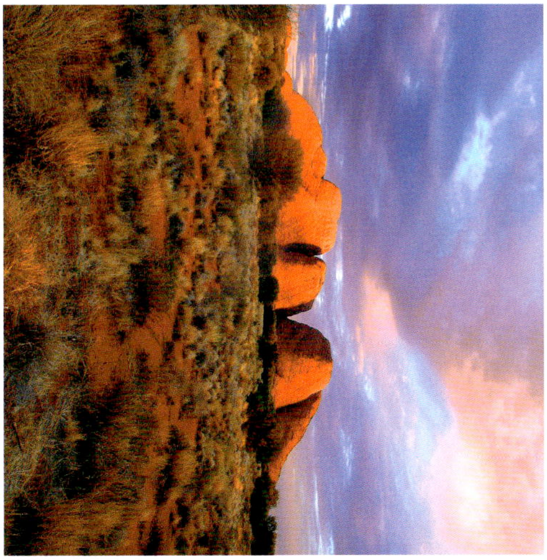

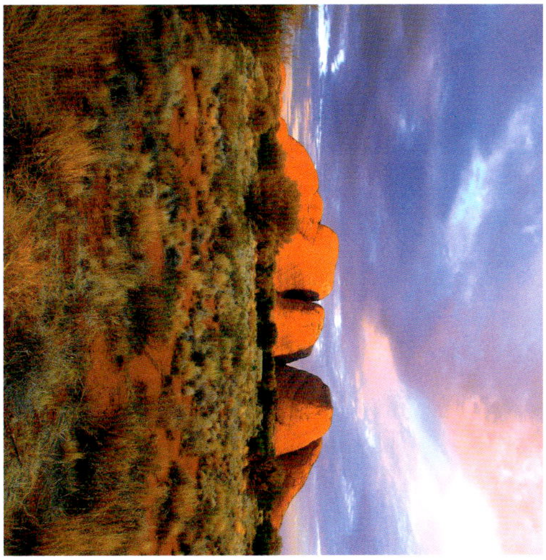

KOALA

Long upstaged by kangaroos, wallabies and emus in the national psyche, koalas came into their own when discovered by overseas visitors who revel in their cuddly touch and gentle nature. Often mistakenly referred to as "bears", these unique tree-living marsupials with their soft grey fur, bulbous nose, bushy ears and beady little eyes eat only selected leaves and seldom drink water. They like to live in secluded high branches, spending long periods perched in precarious positions doing very little.

Koala mothers usually only give birth once a year. Baby is carried in the pouch for six months and then on mother's back for a further six months, which makes them particularly vulnerable to bushfires. Sadly, modern suburban development encroaches on their most precious habitat and they are no longer seen in areas where they were once common. In fact, in much of the country they are considered an endangered species.

Photograph by Ken Duncan

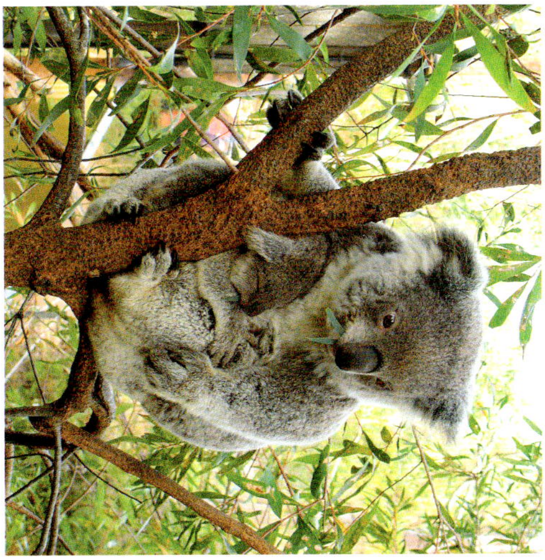
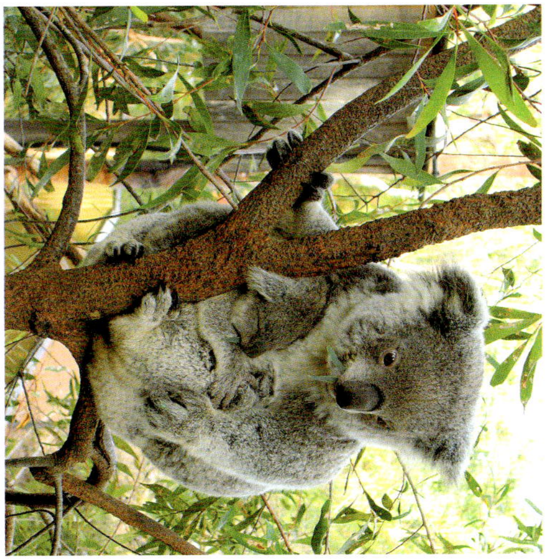

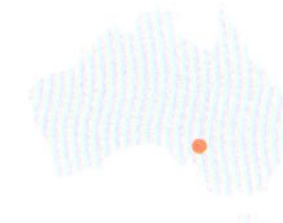

GRASS TREE, FLINDERS RANGES, SA

A grass tree glows in the evening light of the Flinders Ranges, South Australia. There are no sunsets on earth quite like Australian sunsets. Not only does the sky and the country turn every imaginable colour during the magic hour before and after sunset, but the bush is alive with the sounds of native birds and insects. As evening descends, it brings the promise of a good yarn around the campfire, new friendships to be made, a damper, a cup of billy tea and perhaps a camp oven stew or barbecue to be enjoyed.

It has been this way in Australia for thousands of years – indigenous Australians sat by the camp fire, watched the shadows flicker and dance on the red rocks and told stories of ancient times. Modern roads and vehicles have allowed a new generation of Australians to go outback into magical places like the Flinders Ranges and let the Aussie bush fill their senses.

Photograph by Leo Meier

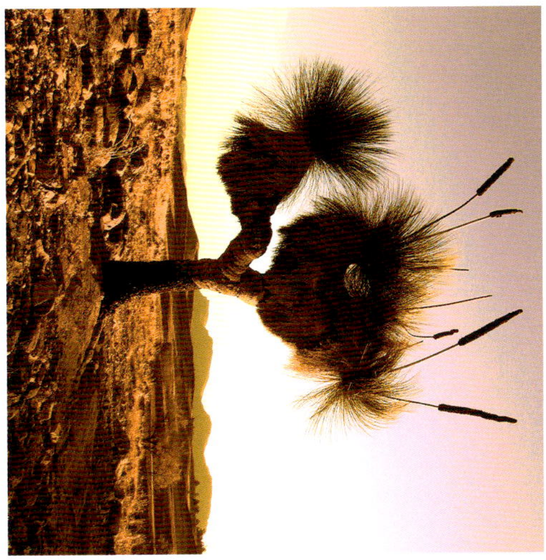

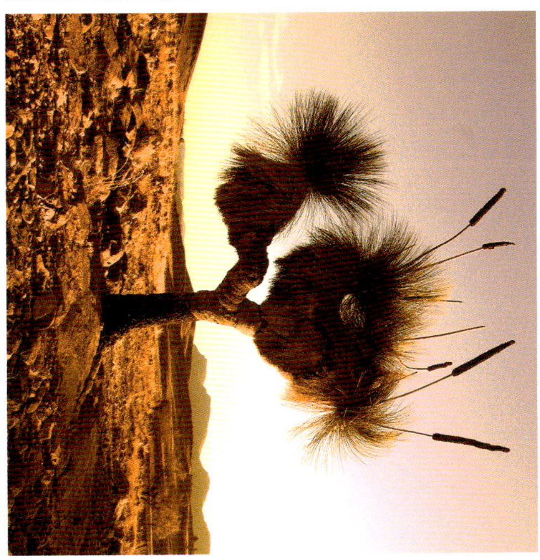

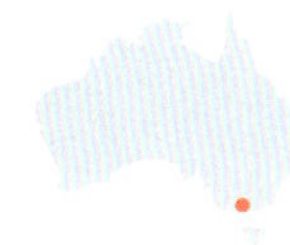

ROWERS, YARRA RIVER, VIC

Melbourne is a city built on traditions and one of the many constants has been the sight of rowers on the Yarra. Here oarsmen clamber out across a slippery deck and ready their slim, arrow-like craft for the test of stamina and strength to come.

The Yarra is the focus of new growth in traditional Melbourne, with the Crown Entertainment Complex, Melbourne Exhibition Centre, Southgate and the Docklands development area taking pride of place along its banks.

This city of 3.5 million people is rated by major travel and lifestyle magazines as one of the most desirable places in the world to live. Its great traditions have been maintained down through the years with a strong arts base and a café society.

Photograph by Ken Duncan

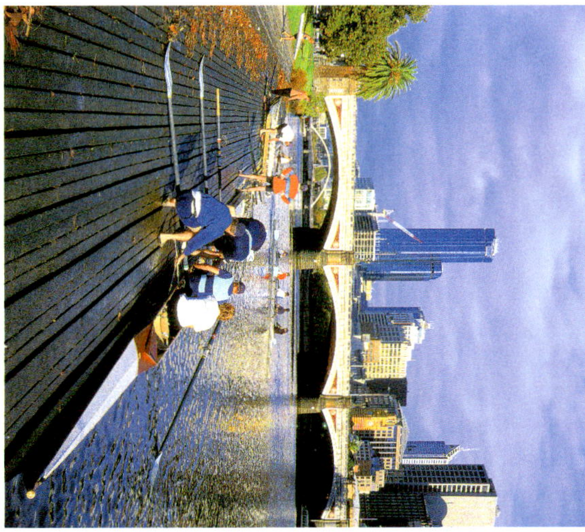

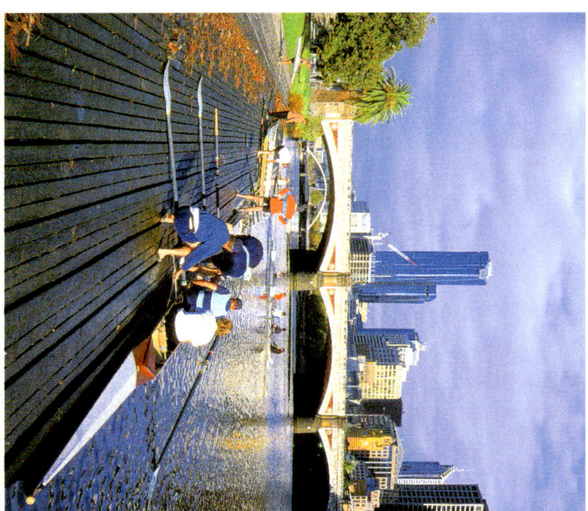

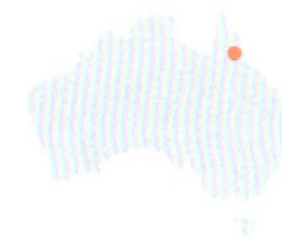

MILLAA MILLAA FALLS, QLD

The tiny town of Millaa Millaa is the centre of waterfall country on the lush Atherton Tableland. Just outside town is the easily accessible Millaa Millaa Falls, the most famous of the falls in this part of Queensland. This photo was taken in a time of extreme drought, but the water still flows. In the area around the town there are 22 waterfalls, many of which can be seen on the mostly sealed 15 kilometre Waterfalls Circuit.

The wet climate and the relatively recent volcanic activity in this region, have combined to create an exceptional setting in which a multitude of streams permanently cascade into rock pools below. All the waterfalls in this area are shrouded by thick, tropical vegetation, which means you can generally hear them before you see them. These are places of tranquil solitude where the sound of cascading water and the call of jungle birds are all you need to hear.

The last volcanic eruptions occurred just a few thousand years ago and local Aboriginal legends tell of red fire in the sky.

Photograph by Ken Duncan

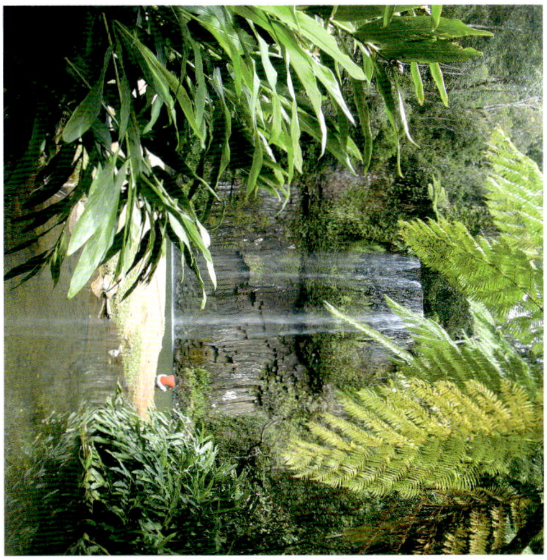

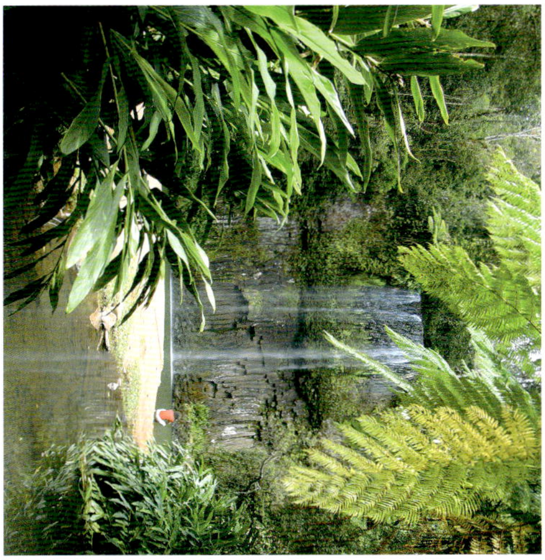

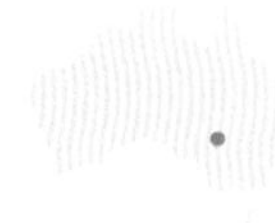

SILVERTON PUB, NSW

Just 27 kilometres north of the outback NSW capital of Broken Hill, Silverton boomed when silver chlorides were discovered in the 1880s and the pub dates from that period. The town had a second boom in recent years when it was the setting for movies such as *Mad Max II, Young Einstein* and *The Adventures of Priscilla Queen of the Desert*, to name just a few. Many visiting movie stars have enjoyed a cold ale or two at the bar of the famous old pub. Despite the fact that Silverton is long past its roaring days and is almost a ghost town, the pub is thriving thanks to the thousands of visitors who pass through.

Similar country towns dot much of western NSW and are often forgotten in the tourist rush to get to Central or Northern Australia. There are many rewards to be had in visiting outback NSW – the friendly people, the lack of hustle and bustle and the quiet solitude of it all. Most Australians live in the city, but many families can trace their history back to such places. It is part of the tie that binds the city to the outback forever.

Photograph by Ken Duncan

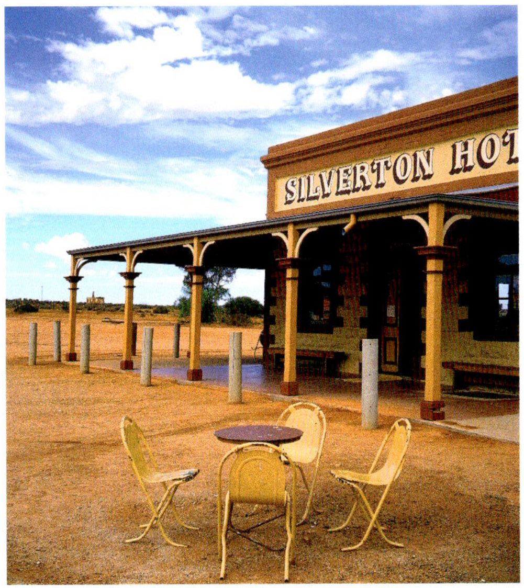
SILVERTON HO
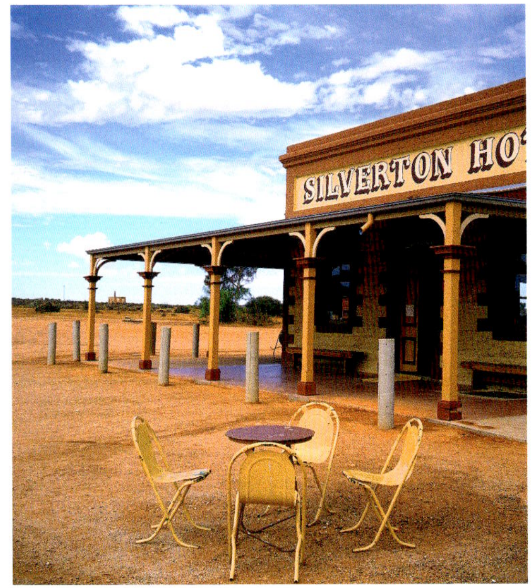
SILVERTON HO

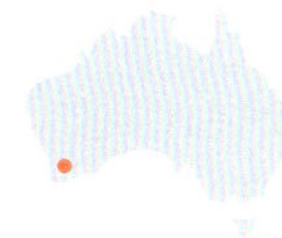

WAVE ROCK, HYDEN, WA

A perfect wave frozen in time, far from the nearest ocean beach. Wave Rock is such a perfect structure that if you looked up to see a surfboard rider passing by you would not be surprised. The lone viewer in the photo demonstrates the enormity of the formation. This ancient granite sculpture is more than 15 metres high and 100 metres long and the bands of colour on the wave are caused by algae.

Wave Rock has become a major tourist attraction in recent times, complete with coffee shop, caravan park and other attractions. However, it is the unique rocks people come to see – distinct granite formations such as Hippo's Yawn, The Breakers, The Humps and The Falls. Mulka's Cave, also in the vicinity, features an interesting display of ancient Aboriginal rock art. Hyden is located 350 kilometres east of Perth in the semi-arid wheat belt.

Photograph by Franz Miller

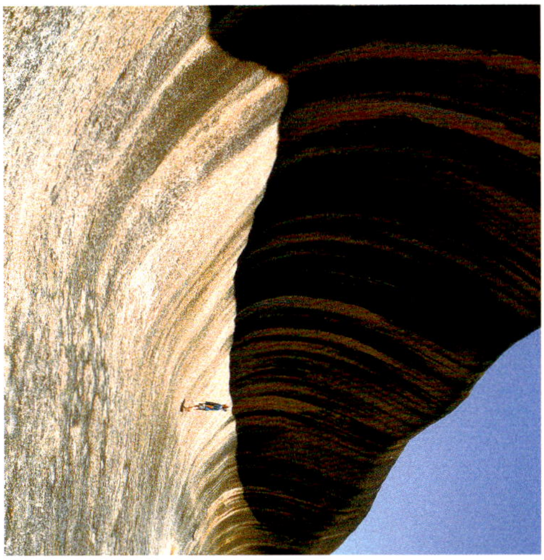

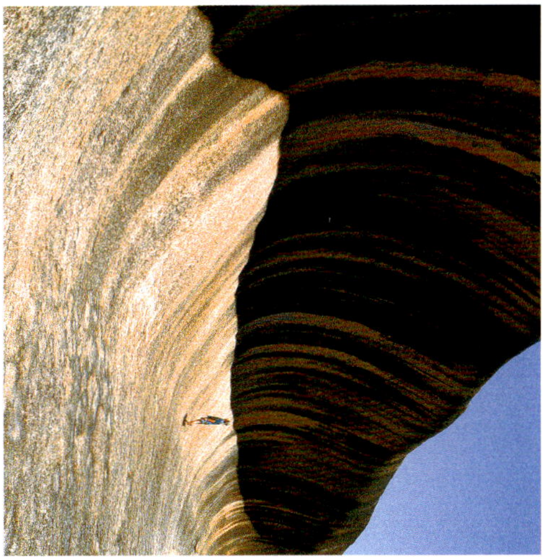

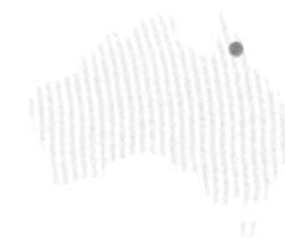

FIG TREE, DAINTREE RAINFOREST, QLD

Giant fig trees with their amazing root systems are a highlight of any visit to the Daintree Rainforest north of Cairns. They are just one of more than a thousand tree species listed in the area. The Daintree is regarded as the oldest continuous rainforest on earth and is of immense biological importance. Many examples of flora and fauna found in this place occur nowhere else in the world yet sadly, much of the area is still under threat from clearing for farms and development in the future.

Sit for a while in this place and listen to the sound of the rainforest creatures all around. The call of the forest birds, the buzz of the insect life, the gentle stream bubbling over the rocks below and perhaps, in the hills to the west, the rumbling of a building thunderstorm.

Photograph by Franz Miller

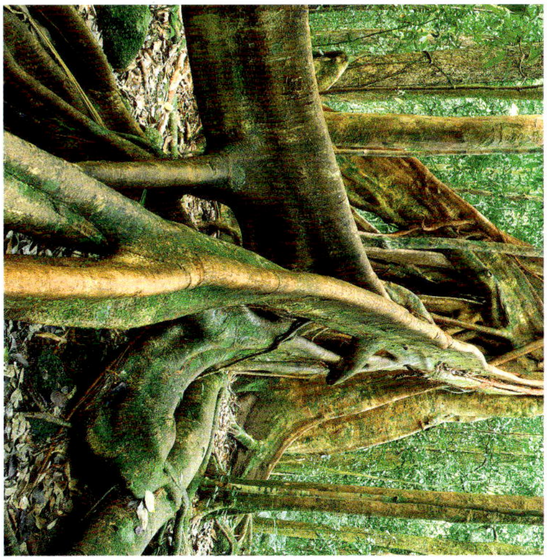

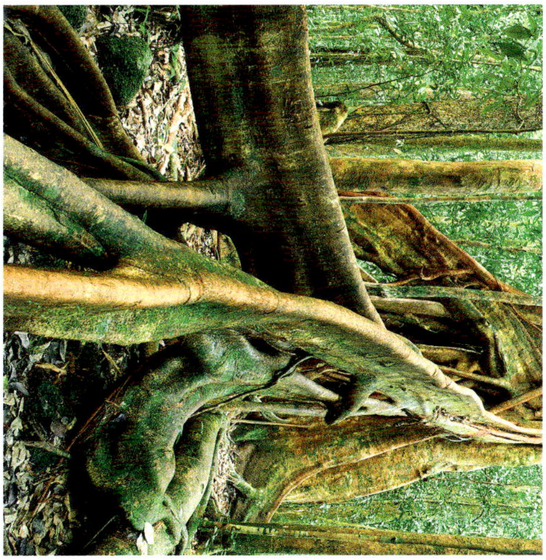

PINK ROADHOUSE, OODNADATTA, SA

The locals always give you a warm welcome at Australia's most unusual road stop, The Pink Roadhouse at Oodnadatta. The tiny town's fame far exceeds its size and it seems to strike a chord as being the "real outback" to many Australians.

It is an old rail town 1000 kilometres north of Adelaide and, apart from the famous roadhouse, the grandest structure in town is the sandstone railway station, built in 1890. The old Ghan train used to shake, rattle and roll its way through town bound for Alice Springs from Adelaide in the days before the modern route was moved further west. Now it is an isolated haven of oddness and wry Aussie outback humour, crowned by this amazing establishment.

In the area is Witjira National Park, gateway to the awe-inspiring Simpson Desert. Dalhousie Springs and the ruins of its early pastoral station are another highlight. In Aboriginal terms, the name Oodnadatta originated from "yellow blossom of the mulga", although these days it may well be pink blossom, judging by the paint job.

Photograph by Leo Meier

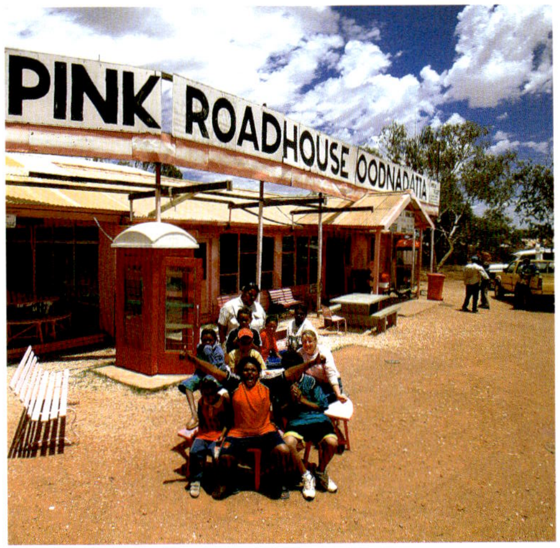
PINK ROADHOUSE OODNADATTA
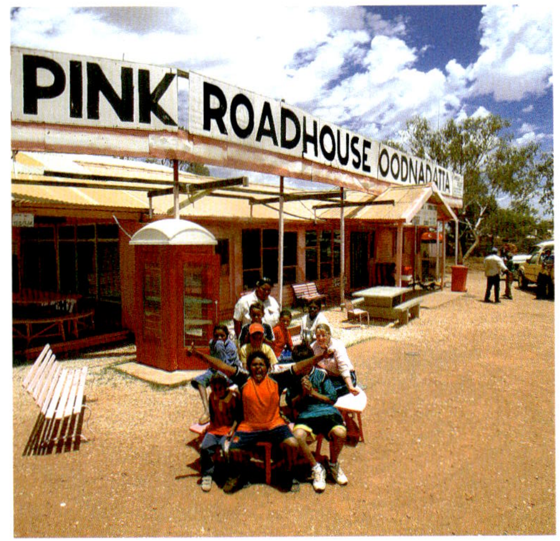
PINK ROADHOUSE OODNADATTA

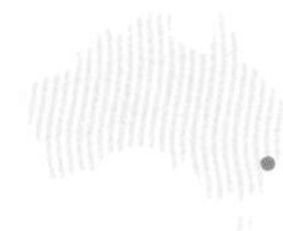

ERIC THE CROCODILE, REPTILE PARK, NSW

If you plan to smile at Eric the crocodile, make sure you do it at a safe distance. A star resident of the Australian Reptile Park near Gosford NSW, Eric allows thousands of people to see a crocodile up close and personal without the dangers involved in a wild encounter with one of these formidable creatures. He may appear tame at times, but crocodiles are unpredictable creatures that should be treated with extreme caution at all times.

Saltwater or estuarine crocodiles inhabit the north of Australia from below Broome in the west to north of Fraser Island in the east. They can be found far from the ocean, holed up in billabongs and quiet creeks, when the waters of the wet season recede and cut off their retreat.

Photograph by Ken Duncan

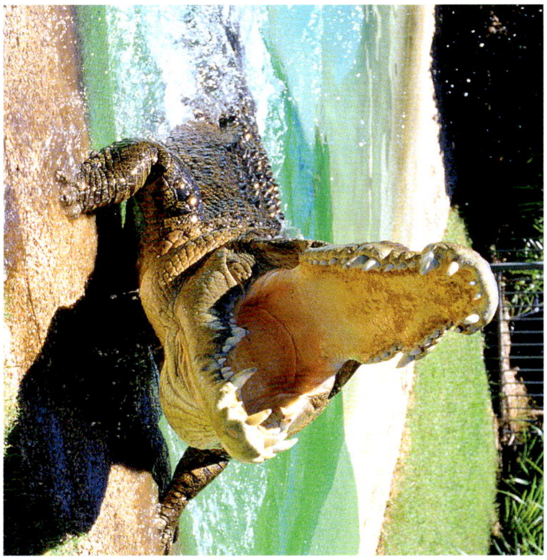

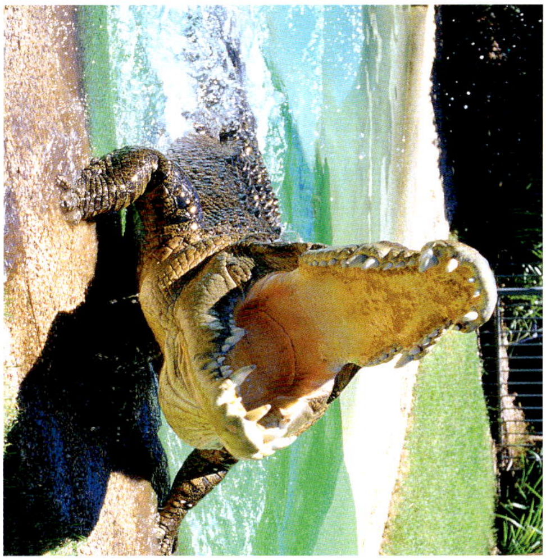

LORD HOWE ISLAND, NSW

The brooding blue twin peaks of Mt Lidgbird and Mt Gower make the perfect backdrop to Lord Howe Island's beautiful tropical lagoon. Rated one of the most outstanding natural islands in the world, Lord Howe Island is 500 kilometres east of NSW and a million miles from the modern world. It contains some of the rarest flora and fauna on earth. The coral reef around parts of the island is the most southerly of its type in the world, thanks to the warm ocean currents that stream down from the Coral Sea.

Lord Howe Island has a laid-back lifestyle all of its own and the modern world seems to have passed it by. Most visitors stay in guesthouses and only a limited number of people are allowed on the island each year. This means it is never crowded and you can find solitude and great beauty along the many deserted roads and tracks.

If you go, take the time to sit on a quiet headland under the Norfolk pines and gaze out to sea. You will get a new perspective on what an awesome place this world can be.

Photograph by Ken Duncan

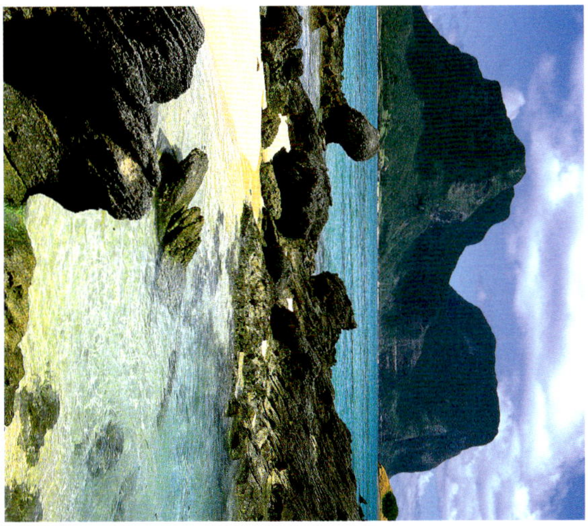

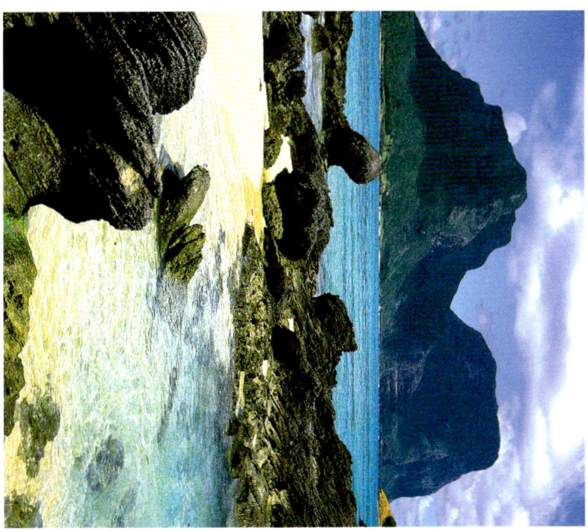

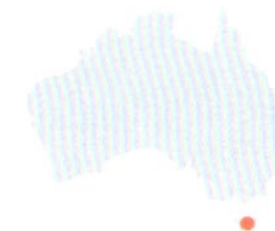

KITCHEN HUT, CRADLE MOUNTAIN, TAS

A refuge and sanctuary for generations of walkers, Kitchen Hut stands at the foot of Cradle Mountain, defiant against the Tasmanian elements. Similar huts are dotted throughout the national park and save lives when the weather changes dramatically and dangerously. The height of the upper door is proof of how high the snow can get in these places.

The most famous walk in this area is the Overland Track which winds entrancingly through beautiful emerald-green forest and across stark moorlands carved by glaciers. Walkers need to be aware at all times of the potential dangers in such places. However, the joy of coming across Bennett's wallabies grazing on a clearing, watching pademelons hop by, or coming face to face with a wombat, are reward enough for the hard life on the trail.

Photograph by Ken Duncan

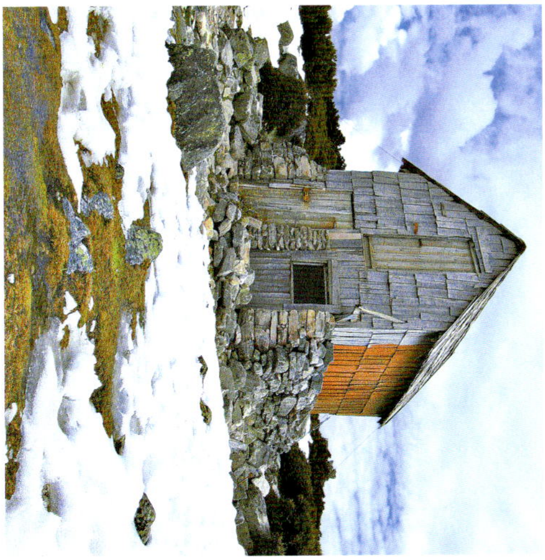

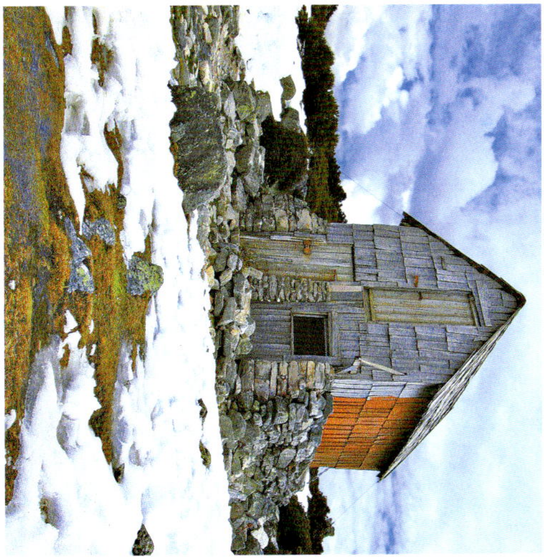

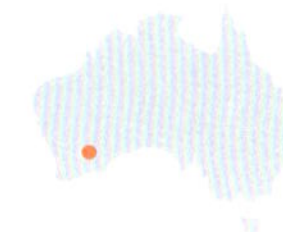

SKIMPIES, SAMANTHA AND SARAH, KALGOORLIE, WA

The mining capital of Kalgoorlie still retains some of its wild edges from the roaring days. More than 30 pubs abound, filled with miners and workers enjoying a cleansing ale, and each has its own unique flavour. Yet, there is beauty to be found in this desert city. Beautiful young girls clad in skimpy outfits serve drinks behind the bar, hence the name “skimpies”. Here Sarah and Samantha take a break from work outside The Exchange Hotel, one of the most famous pubs in Kalgoorlie.

Modern day Kalgoorlie has managed to combine its historic past with newer developments and hopefully it will always have that rugged frontier atmosphere that sets it apart. It produces half of Australia’s gold and the nearby Golden Mile is considered the richest square mile of gold-bearing ore on earth.

Photograph by Ken Duncan

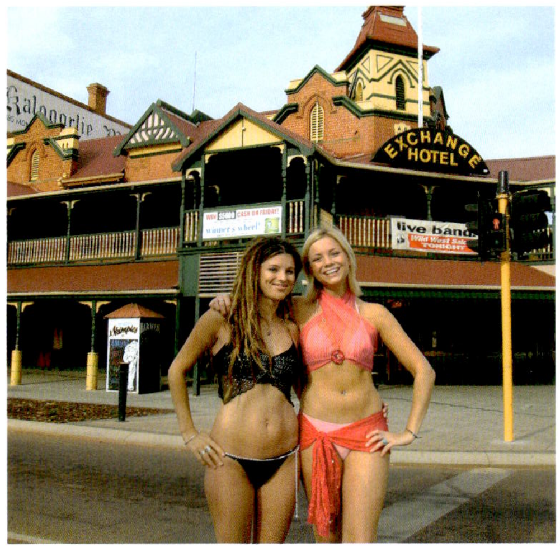
EXCHANGE HOTEL
live band

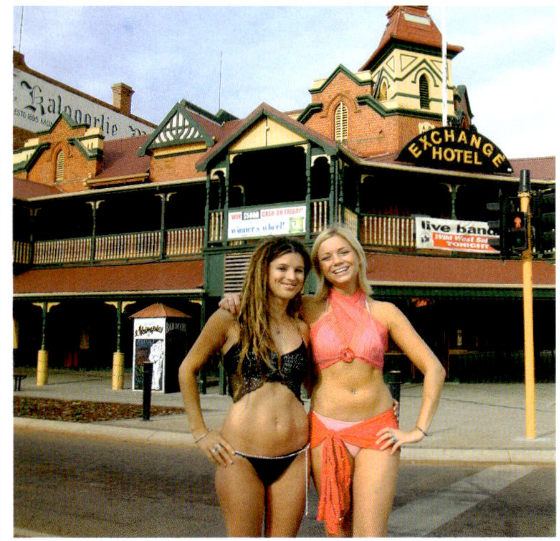
EXCHANGE HOTEL
live band

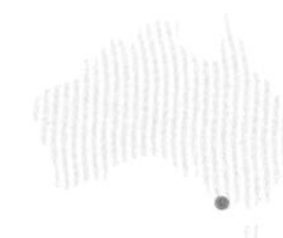

TWELVE APOSTLES, PORT CAMPBELL NATIONAL PARK, VIC

The first rays of morning capture the dramatic coastline of southern Victoria and light up The Twelve Apostles. For eons they have stood steadfast against the huge seas that boom up from the Great Southern Ocean.

Carved out of the cliffs by the wind and wild surf, each of the natural sandstone statues has a design and character of its own. Adding to the grandeur are the dramatic high cliffs and narrow beaches along this section of Port Campbell National Park.

The fact that there is no large town nearby simply increases the mystique of The Twelve Apostles – they simply exist just a few metres off the road at the end of flowing paddocks. A network of viewing platforms makes it easy for visitors to enjoy the vista and wait for the magical sunrise or sunset to set it all aglow. This awesome display is at the western end of the Great Ocean Road, arguably Australia's best cliff drive.

Photograph by Franz Miller

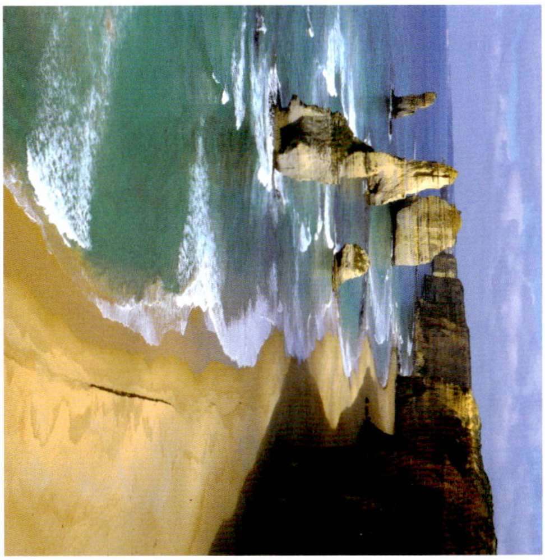

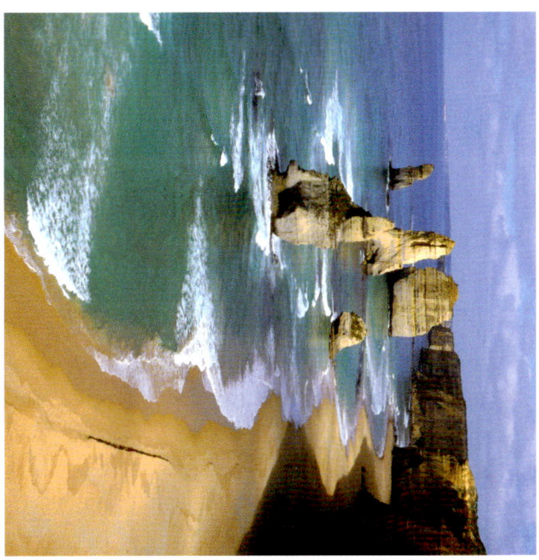

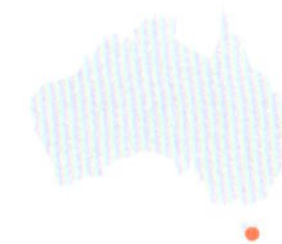

TASMANIAN DEVIL, TAS

Not the most endearing native creatures, the nocturnal devils are noisy and rugged little marsupials with huge teeth and a high-pitched scream. When competing with each other they have a scream rather like a circular saw and can adopt a threatening pose, but generally do not fight. Early settlers, unnerved by the night-time screams of Australia's only pitch-black marsupial, nicknamed it devil. The settlers then set about giving it a terrible reputation, claiming it was a ruthless predator of livestock, killing sheep, calves and dogs. It was even claimed the devil would attack people protecting their stock.

All this has been proved untrue in modern times. Although the devil is a carnivore, it is a scavenger, entirely dependent on the carrion of dead animals. This means it is actually a benefit to agriculture because it removes carcasses from the forest. However it is best to leave them alone and keep your fingers away, because their sharp teeth could easily amputate a digit.

Photograph by Ken Duncan

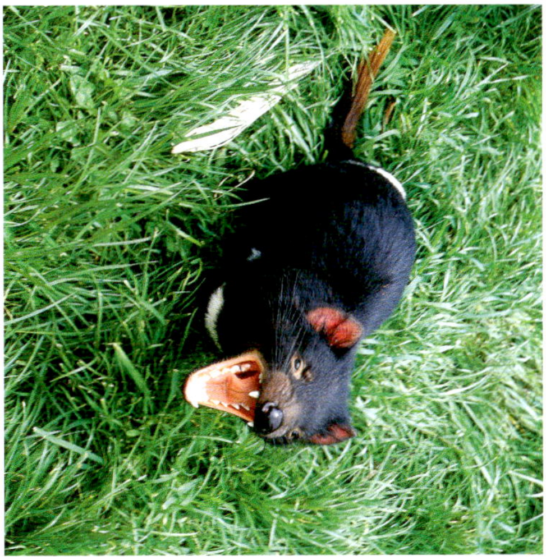

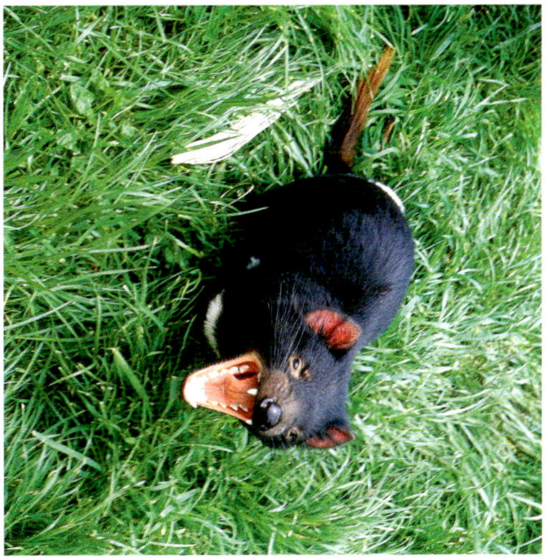

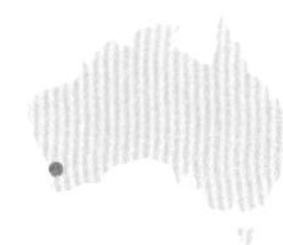

KINGS PARK, PERTH, WA

Perth is one of the most isolated major cities on earth, yet this little girl seems to sum up its glowing future. Many Australians have looked west to Perth and been drawn to its reputation as a wealthy, booming city which holds a rich promise of a new life.

This scene is taken from Kings Park, a major sanctuary in the city enjoyed by locals and visitors alike. The 400 hectares of natural bushland with man-made lakes, gardens, children's playgrounds and many interesting walks, provides an appealing contrast to the bustling city nearby.

Perth, set beside the Swan River, with a population of almost 1.5 million people, is a fascinating blend of contemporary and historic buildings. To the south-west is the historic port of Fremantle, which, since hosting the America's Cup in 1987, has taken on a cosmopolitan air.

Photograph by Ken Duncan

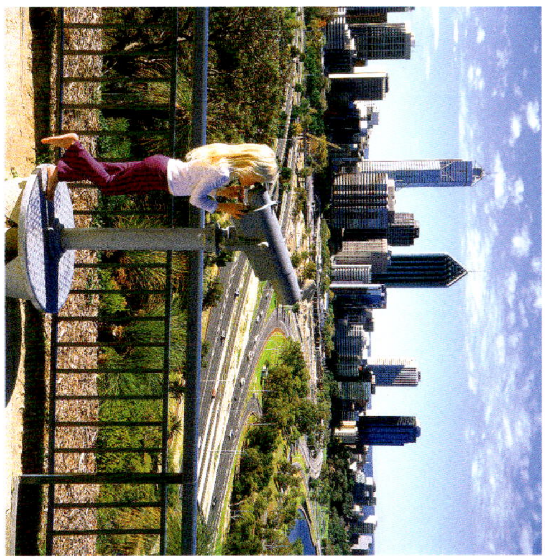

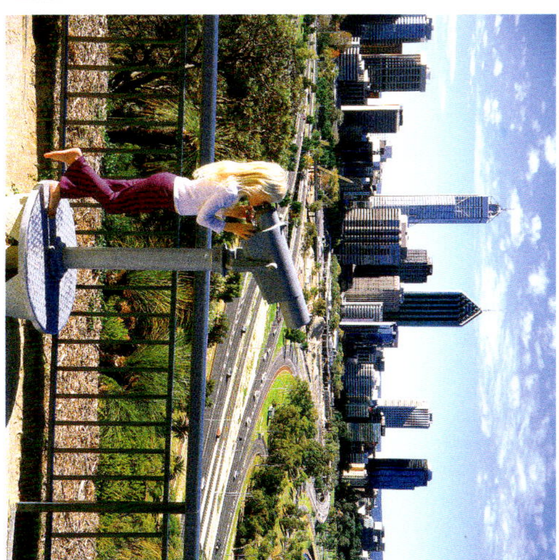

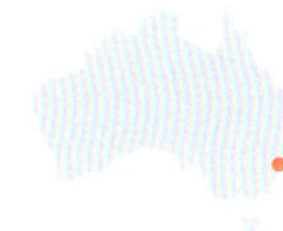

AUTUMN, MATCHAM, NSW

On this crisp, clear autumn morning in Matcham you could be standing in a forest in New England or northern Europe. The leaves are turning a golden orange as the weather grows cooler, giving a spectacular display of colour only nature can provide. In fact, you are just over one hour from the bustle of downtown Sydney. This photo illustrates how easy it is in Australia to escape the city life.

Matcham is just one of many secluded valleys that dot the NSW Central Coast. The blend of rural solitude and wild ocean beaches gives the coast a unique lifestyle. Within five minutes of just about anywhere you can be walking on a country road or lazing on your own patch of sand.

Photograph by Ken Duncan

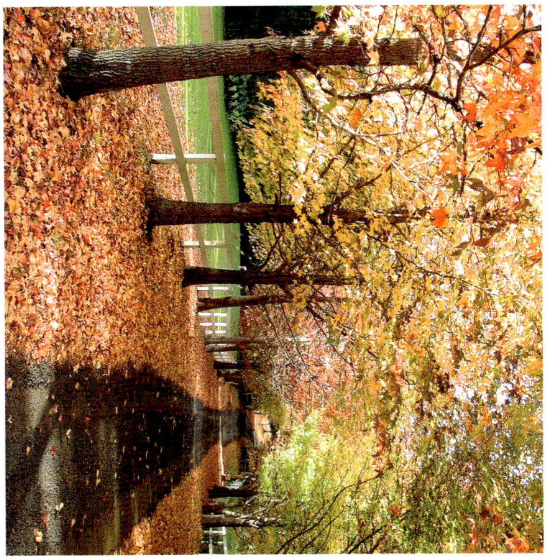

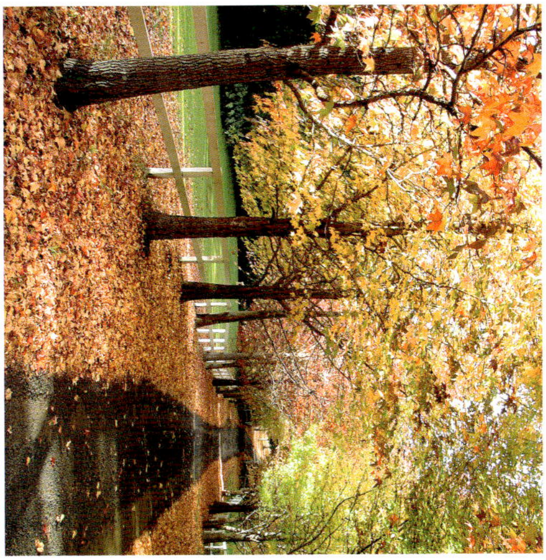

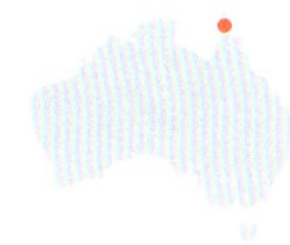

CANAL CREEK, CAPE YORK, QLD

Much of Cape York is a rugged, little-known area of wide plains, pockets of rainforest and hundreds of uninhabited islands. This is the region of the Wet Season, where storm clouds build up for weeks on end until finally the weather cracks and a deluge of rainfall turns vast areas into inland lakes and swamps.

Canal Creek is at the far end of the Cape and a visit to Split Falls is a must for any visitor travelling north to Bamaga. The creek derives its name from a canal-like stream-bed which is so precisely carved and so straight it seems to be man-made.

Nearby Elliot Falls offers a popular campsite with smallish clearings in the thick bush connected by short tracks. Sitting around the campfire and swapping travel tales with newfound friends is one of the delights of travelling in the outback.

Photograph by Nancy Moxom

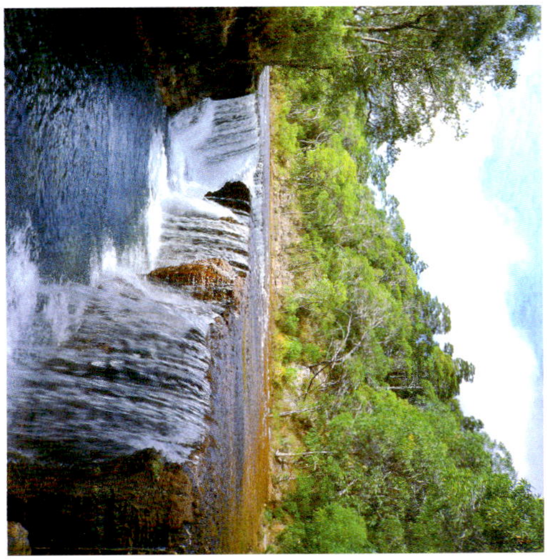

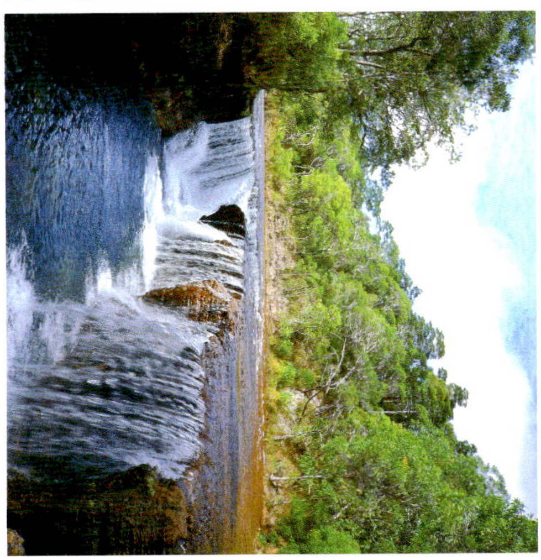

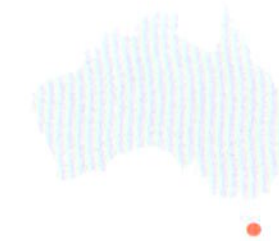

RICHMOND BRIDGE, TAS

You could be excused for thinking you are somewhere in rural England, but this is in fact Richmond Bridge in Tasmania. Pause for a while on the green riverbank and enjoy a tranquil interlude, complete with a family of ducks going about their business. This peaceful setting belies the sad history of the famous bridge built by convicts under dreadful conditions between 1823 and 1825. Local legends tell of frequent sightings of the ghost of an overseer who was murdered by enraged convicts.

This impressive construction is Australia's oldest surviving freestone bridge and its perfect lines and exceptional stonework are a tribute to the people who designed and built it. Richmond, just 26 kilometres north-east of Hobart, features many convict-built buildings dating from the 1830s or earlier. These include Richmond Gaol (1825) and a number of churches.

Photograph by Ken Duncan

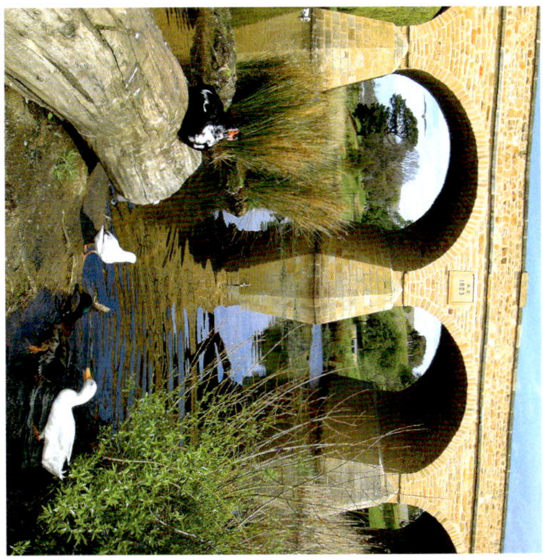

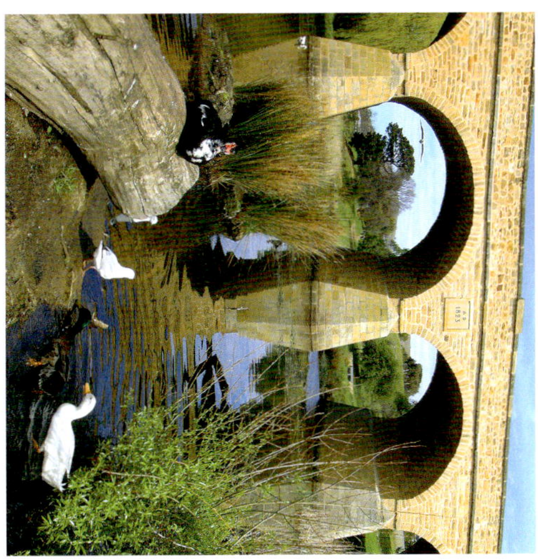

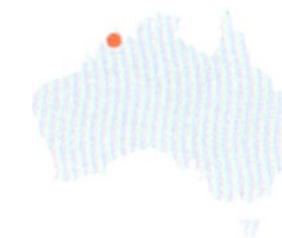

MITCHELL FALLS, KIMBERLEY, WA

The vast Kimberley region of Western Australia is one of the most isolated and awesomely beautiful places on earth. This photo of Mitchell Falls, perched atop the Mitchell Plateau, perfectly sums up the rugged grandeur of this area.

The photo was taken in the dry, cooler months, yet it gives an indication of the variation between the wet and dry seasons in the north-west. At the peak of the wet, the river becomes an amazing surge of bucking, crashing whitewater filling the gorge in an overwhelming display of power. In the dry, it spills down in a series of giant cascades, interspersed with rock pools and the falls can be reached overland by 4WD vehicle.

Similar falls are found along the Kimberley coast – wild places where huge rivers drop dramatically down gorges as they near the coast. It is possible to travel by boat from the ocean right to the foot of many of these waterfalls. Along the way you will pass through immense sandstone valleys and wild hills teeming with wildlife. There is virtually no evidence of man having been there, apart from the occasional cave painting or adventurer's boat.

Photograph by Franz Miller

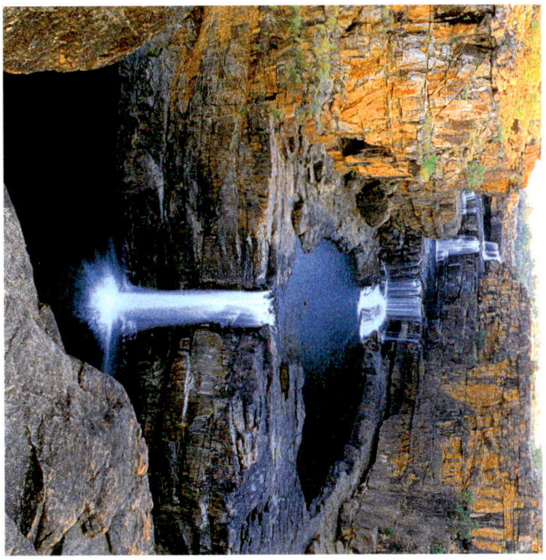

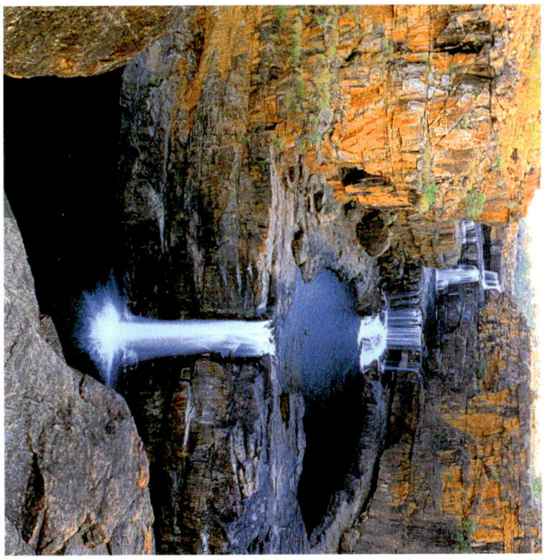

HEART REEF, THE GREAT BARRIER REEF, QLD

This tiny heart-shaped reef is one of the more famous sights along the Great Barrier Reef. In the background floats one of the many pontoons that act as home base during the day for visitors to the reef. Strung out like giant opals in a turquoise setting, the Great Barrier Reef is an amazing sight from the air. It stretches for more than 2000 kilometres from the tip of Cape York to almost Fraser Island.

The reef itself is a place of subtle variations. In the tropical north, it is older and better developed with a wide range of species. The sea life has changed little from ancient times because of the lack of stress from outside factors. It is a world of its own beneath the waves.

Man can only visit such places briefly to experience the myriad colours and shapes of marine life and bask in the warm waters. Amazingly, the Great Barrier Reef is the only living thing on Earth visible from outer space.

Photograph by Ken Duncan

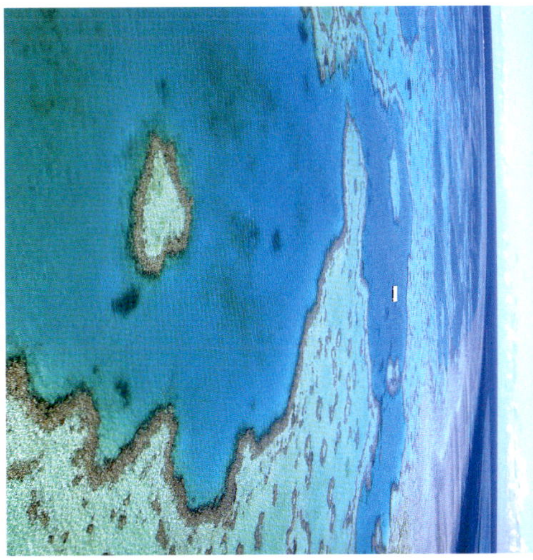

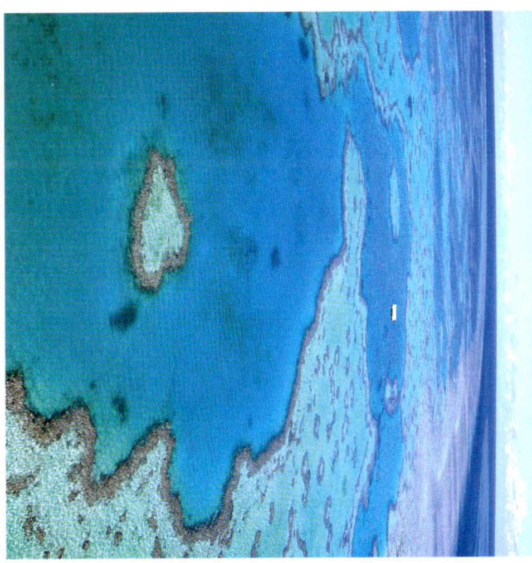

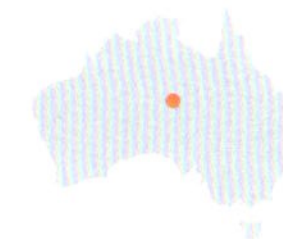

TREPHINA GORGE NATURE PARK, NT

East of Alice Springs near Ross River Homestead is Trapinka Sands, a quiet, isolated part of Trephina Gorge Nature Park. Here you can sit and listen to the sounds of silence as Aboriginal people did in times gone by. The dramatic MacDonnell Ranges, stretching east and west of Alice Springs for hundreds of kilometres, feature this and many other famous gorges. To the west of Alice Springs lie Stanley Chasm, Simpson's Gap and Ormiston Gorge. The eastern ranges are less frequently visited by tourists and you are more likely to find a secluded spot. On a perfect day, the only sounds you might hear are the call of birds that come seeking the life-giving waters of the rock pool and the murmur of the desert breeze in the tree branches. The colours change as the sun moves across the sky. In the late afternoon you can feel what it must have been like to sit by an ancient campfire in such places and watch the flame shadows dancing on the walls.

Photograph by Ray Moxom

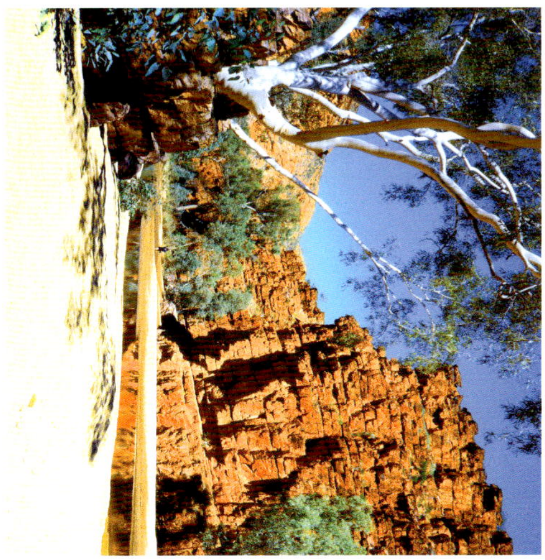

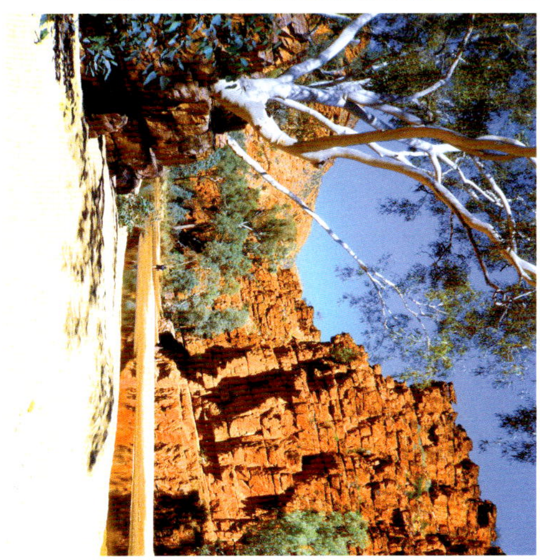

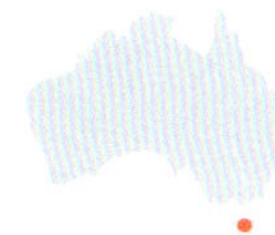

DOVE LAKE, CRADLE MOUNTAIN REFLECTIONS, TAS

Dove Lake epitomises the grandeur of the World Heritage-listed Cradle Mountain–Lake St Clair National Park in central Tasmania. This area is the closest Australia comes to the wild alps of New Zealand, Europe and America. It is a region of great variation, ranging from emerald-green forests – carpeted end to end in moss and lichens – to high mountain regions blasted by blizzards. The wild climate means the scene is ever changing, with blue sky suddenly replaced by low clouds racing in to shroud the area with misty rain. It is a land of wild beech and myrtle forests, King Billy pines and wildflowers galore.

Wildlife abounds in this region and visitors are able to spot many types of nocturnal marsupials including the noisy and not so friendly Tasmanian Devils. There is a variety of walking tracks available, ranging from easy to arduous, such as the famous 85 kilometre Overland Track. Near Dove Lake, a visitors' centre and accommodation in the form of Cradle Mountain Lodge bring a touch of modern civilisation into an otherwise harsh environment.

Photograph by Ken Duncan

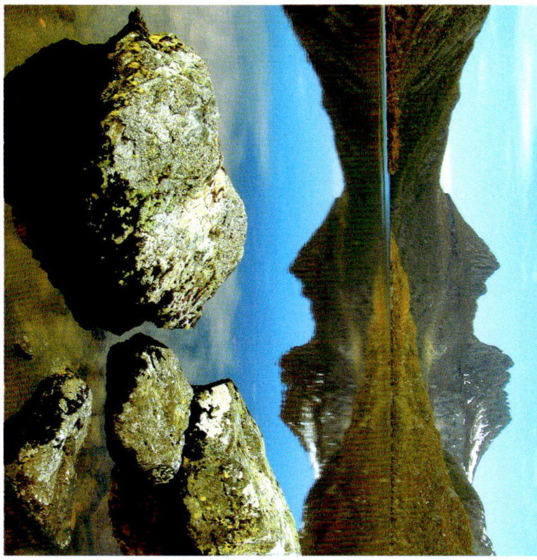

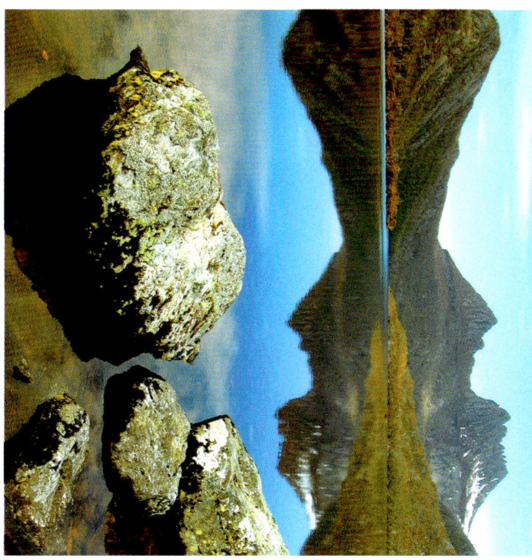

CAPE BYRON LIGHTHOUSE, NSW

The light of creation far surpasses the light of man. It is early morning at Byron Bay, Australia's most easterly point, and the first rays of sunshine herald in a new day. This magic place affords views in every direction and towering over it all is Mt Warning, the remnant of a huge volcano that once dominated this region. On a wet day when thunderclouds climb the sky and shafts of sunlight shoot down on the emerald green farmlands and turquoise ocean beyond, this is an unbeatable place to spend a morning.

In June each year, people come from everywhere to see whales migrating north to their winter quarters in Queensland. Plumes of misty spray to the south announce the arrival of the leviathans of the deep and soon there are pods of whales surging up and over the waves in their never-ending journey of life.

Sheltered below is the town of Byron Bay, a cosmopolitan mix of the well-to-do, surfers, people escaping the city and those just looking for something new in their life.

Photograph by Ken Duncan

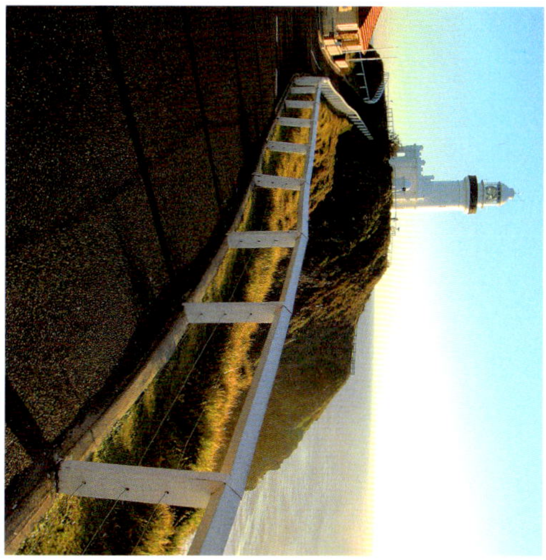

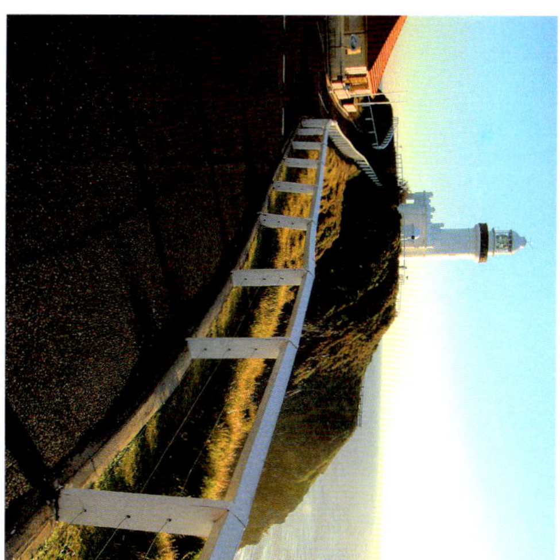

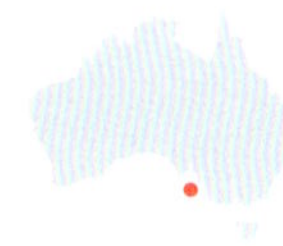

THE REMARKABLES, KANGAROO ISLAND, SA

A sculpture only the hand of creation could mould. The Remarkables on South Australia's Kangaroo Island feature many examples of nature's unique ability to fashion strange and hauntingly beautiful rock forms. Many sculptors would give almost anything to create the scooped indentations and sandpaper texture of these natural works of art, yet here they are – free for all the world to see. Located in Flinders Chase National Park at the far south-west corner of the island, they are exposed to all the fury of the Southern Ocean winds.

Tranquil Kangaroo Island, Australia's third largest island, lies 16 kilometres off the tip of the Fleurieu Peninsula. Its natural beauty shelters a wide variety of Australian animals that have found sanctuary in their traditional native habitat. Koalas, sea lions, kangaroos, wallabies, penguins, seals and even platypus call the island home and live in a relatively safe environment far from the perils of the mainland.

Photograph by Leo Meier

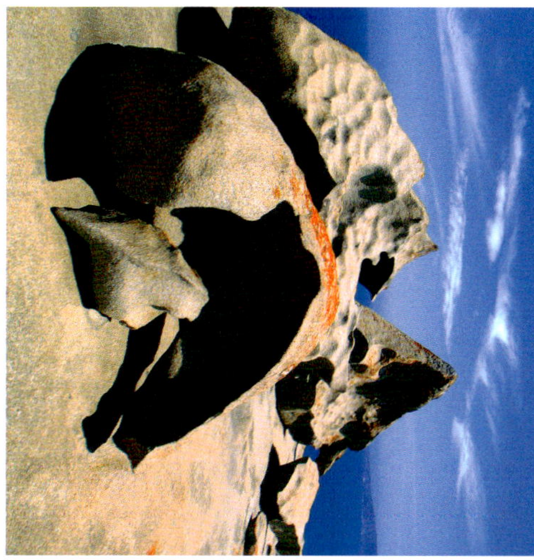

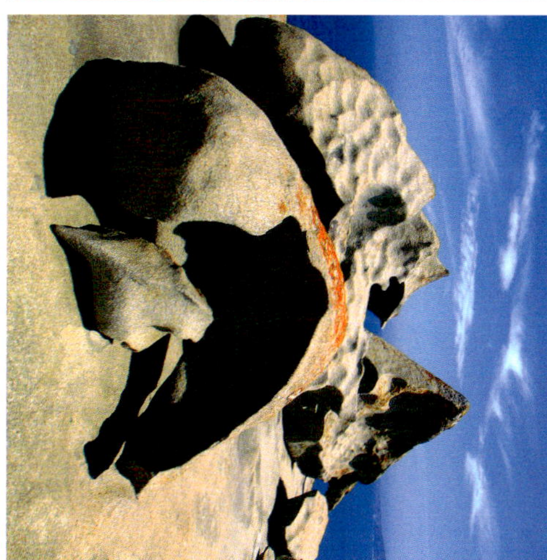

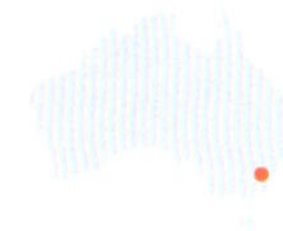

BALLOON FIESTA, CANBERRA, ACT

In the still atmosphere of a crisp Canberra morning, dozens of balloons rise up from the earth to fill the air with dramatic shapes of every colour. During the Balloon Fiesta the skies of the National Capital are alive with these fascinating flying craft. The balloons are launched from the vicinity of old Parliament House on the edge of Lake Burley Griffin. It is a great family occasion, with mums and dads from all over taking their children to see the balloons in flight.

Canberra, one of the world's newest cities, rose from the hills and plains along the Molonglo River west of Queanbeyan early last century to become the nation's major seat of government. In the 1950s, just 25,000 people lived in the city, but today it is home to more than 300,000 people, including many diplomats and other government representatives from around the world.

Photograph by Ken Duncan

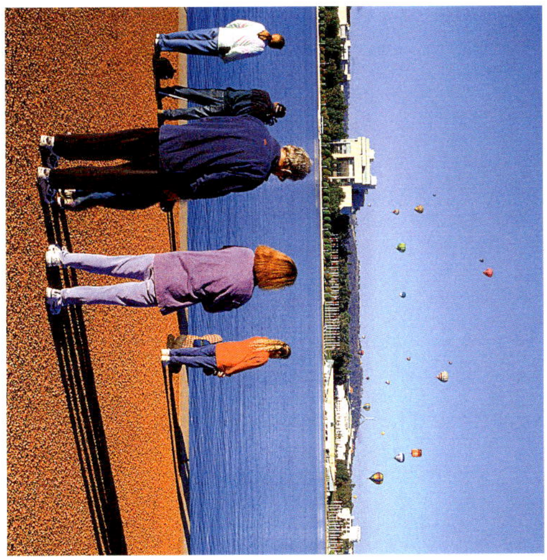

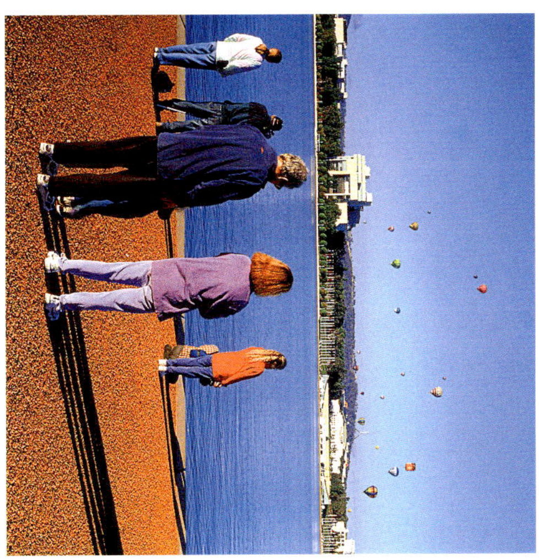

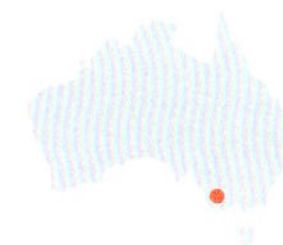

THE BALCONIES, THE GRAMPIANS NATIONAL PARK, VIC

On top of the world! An intrepid hiker on a break takes in the view of a lifetime from The Balconies in the rugged Grampians, north-west Victoria. This ancient mountain range runs through the heart of central Victoria and – seen from a distance – rises like a mirage from the featureless plain. The rough shapes of the blue, grey and brown ranges protect green gullies dotted with ferns, dense forests and cascading waterfalls. There are swamps, secluded creeks and lakes. In the sheer cliffs, caves and rock shelters are found.

This is the home of the Djab Wurrung and Jardwadjali people who left their artwork on the cave walls for modern generations to discover. Much of the area has now been preserved in the Grampians National Park and there is a fascinating network of walking trails and scenic roads to explore.

Photograph by Franz Miller

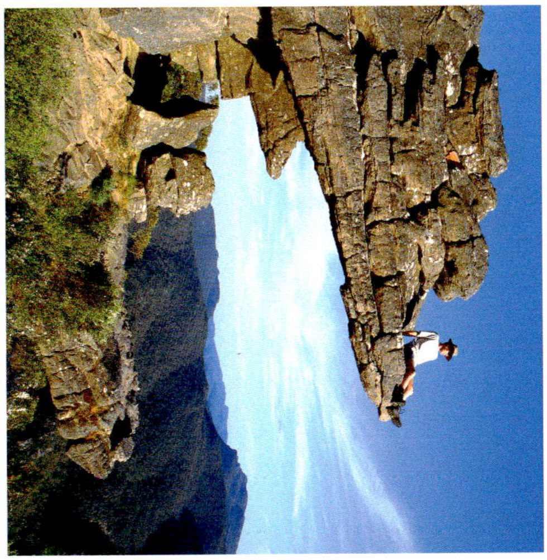

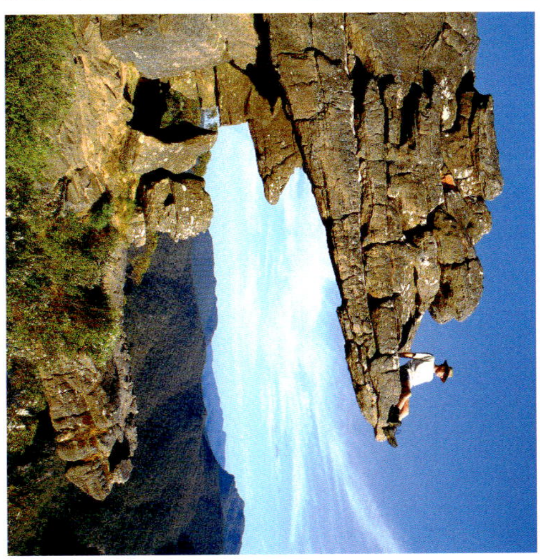

MAGUK FALLS, KAKADU, NT

One of the magical highlights of a visit to Northern Australia is plunging into one of the many rock pools suitable for swimming. Maguk Falls is one such serene place where it is easy to forget the cares of the everyday world and escape into nature at its best. Here water cascades over dramatic cliffs into the large plunge pool below, offering cool, exhilarating relief from the tropical heat. Red rocks – twisted and contorted by the ages – surround the pool, framed by ancient green palms. Maguk Falls is located on Barramundie Creek in the southern section of Kakadu National Park. They are a short 12 kilometre trek by 4WD off the Kakadu Highway near Gungural Recreation Area.

Photograph by Leo Meier

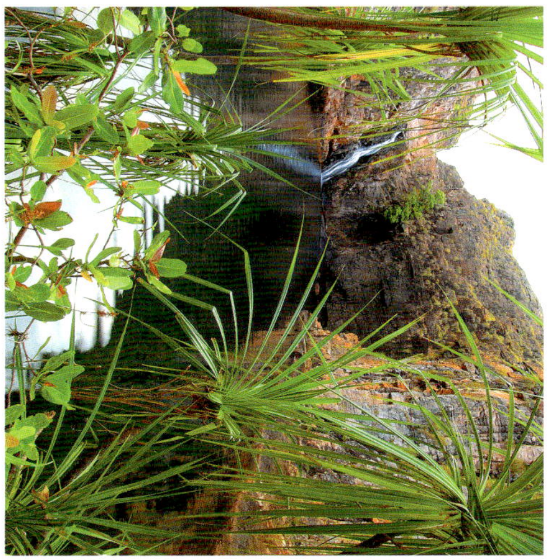

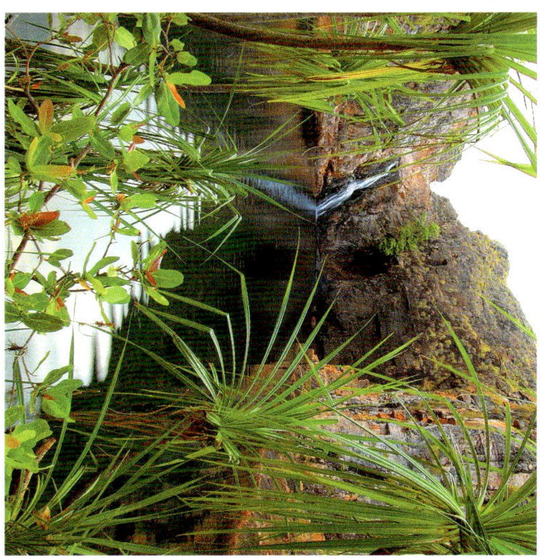

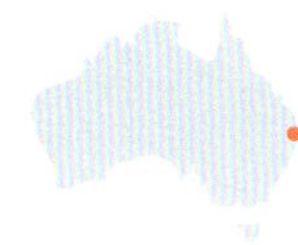

BRISBANE, QLD

The Queensland capital of Brisbane is, like so many Australian cities, a classic mix of old and new. Golden sandstone buildings from the colonial age sit side-by-side with modern glass towers, all glimmering in the warm northern light. What sets Brisbane apart is the tropical foliage, which abounds in the parks and gardens across the city, as well as the unique *Queenslander* homes, built on stilts to beat the heat and the insects.

Brisbane lies along the shores of the Brisbane River, a broad waterway of sweeping curves, which reflects the city skyline in a spectacular lightshow after dark. Today it is home to more than 1.6 million people and is the gateway to the nation's most popular tourist spots, the Gold Coast to the south and the Sunshine Coast to the north.

Just minutes from the bustling city locals can enjoy time out in the beautifully landscaped gardens along the banks of the river or even swim at a man-made beach!

Photograph by Leo Meier

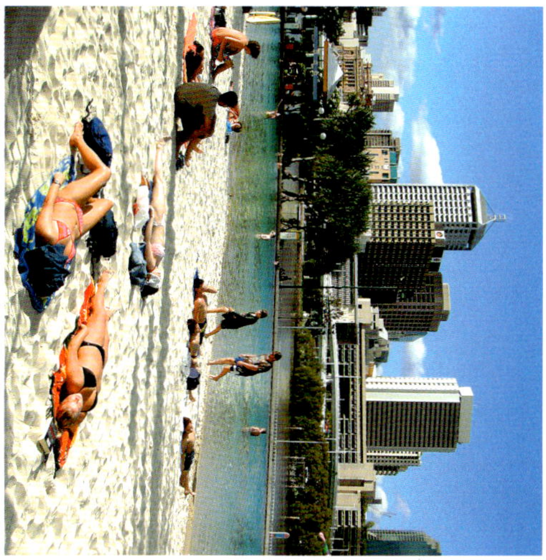

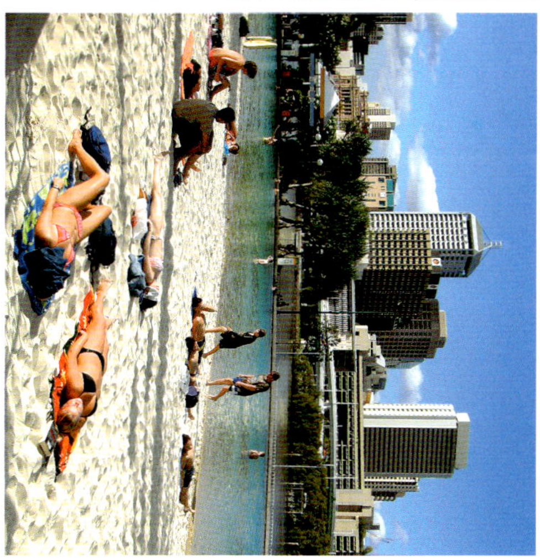

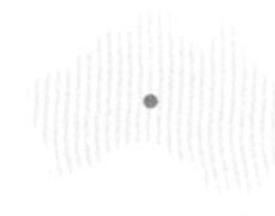

KINGS CANYON, NT

Prepare to have your senses filled completely! This is Kings Canyon, south-west of Alice Springs – a huge gap in the earth's surface that slices the landscape in two. People who visit Kings Canyon are consumed by its size and beauty. Stand on one of the sheer cliff tops and you peer out over an endless sea of sandstone rocks. Sit in the valley below and watch the soaring bluffs continually change colour as the sun passes overhead. Despite its grand scale, it would be easy to travel right by the canyon and not know it was there. One of the more isolated places in Australia, Kings Canyon is north-east of Uluru in Watarrka National Park and was seldom visited until recent times. Now you will find a region of spectacular walks along cliff tops with features like The Lost City and The Garden of Eden. Getting there is quite a drive. Branch off the Lasseter Highway west of Mt Ebenezer Roadhouse or take the unsealed Mereenie Loop Road from Glen Helen Resort. Either way, it is well worth the trip. To the west of the canyon is Kings Canyon Resort, a modern development catering to both campers and accommodated tourists.

Photograph by Franz Miller

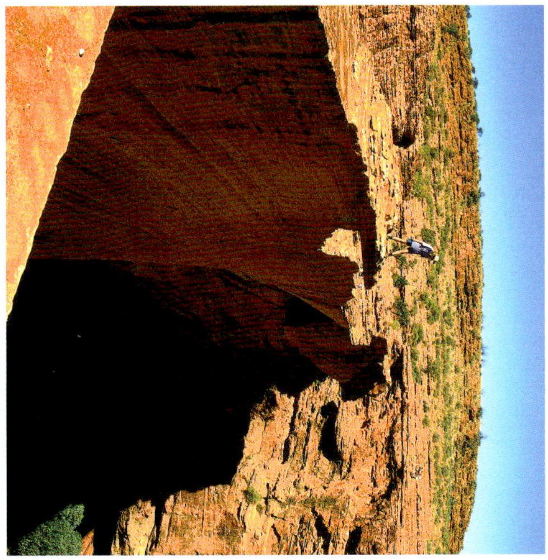

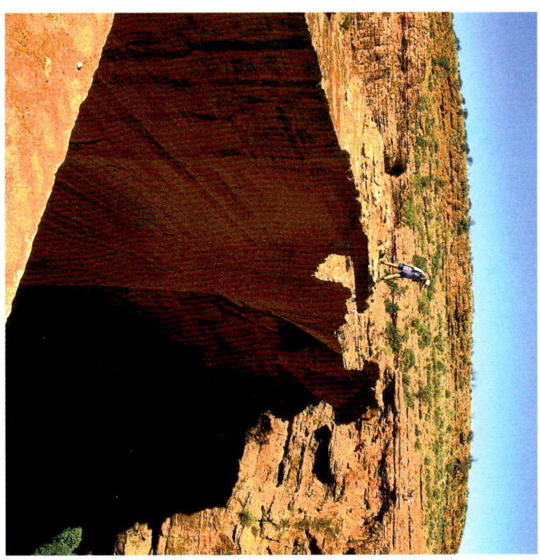

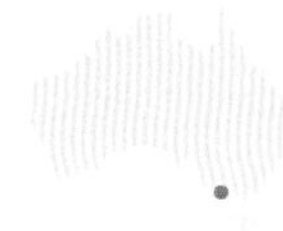

HOPETOUN FALLS, VIC

The roar of water plunging over Hopetoun Falls fills your senses long before you arrive at the secluded valley over which they reign. Located in Otway Reserves Park, in the wild ranges north-west of Apollo Bay, the falls drop 20 metres into a valley shrouded in rainforest and ferns. Mosses and lichens cling to the rocks and overhanging branches by the stream, and the whole scene always seems to be moist. Nearby is the picturesque Aire Valley Reserve with its picnic facilities and pleasant views.

The Otway Ranges are home to Australia's unique southern temperate rainforest, as well as a world of giant ferns, busy streams bubbling over moss-covered rocks and huge trees that climb forever. To the east lie the seaside resort towns of Torquay, Anglesea, Lorne and Apollo Bay, while to the west is the rugged coastline of The Twelve Apostles and Port Campbell National Park.

Photograph by Ken Duncan

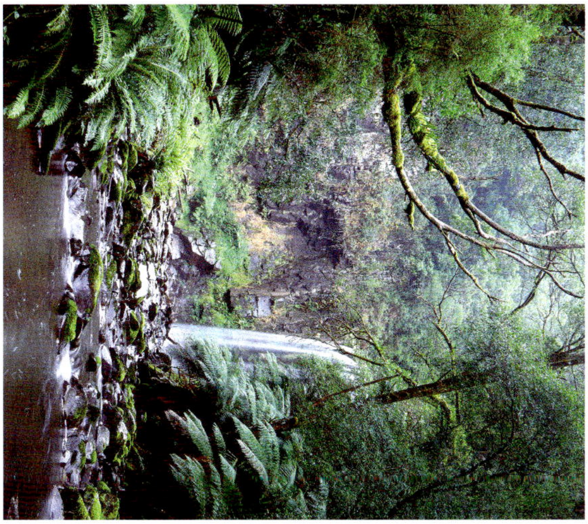

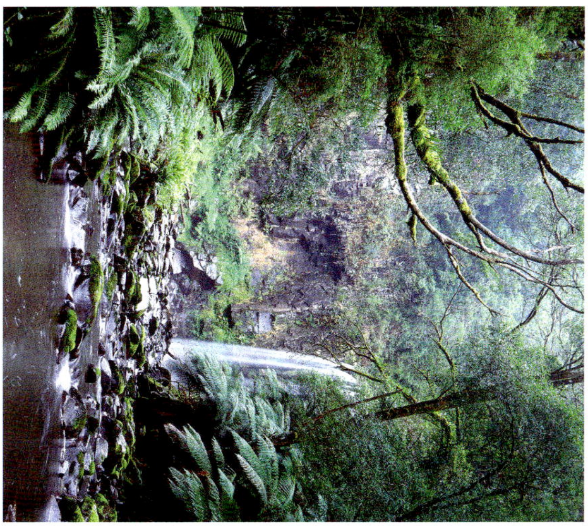

SURFERS PARADISE, TIGER MOTH, QLD

Australia's most popular tourist destination, the Gold Coast, takes on a magic all of its own when viewed from the air. Here a vintage Tiger Moth drones its way north-west on a tourist flight across the Broadwater. Beneath lies traditional Southport, the original town in this part of the coast and beyond is the young upstart, Surfers Paradise, which compares favourably with any beachside tourist resort on earth. Surfers is framed by the Pacific Ocean and the Nerang River, with its multi-million-dollar developments. This combination of man-made structures and nature provides spectacular views from many vantage points, day and night.

Just half a century ago this was a little-known backwater of Queensland with wild sand hills and a few cottages scattered here and there. Today more than a quarter of a million people call it home and millions of people visit each year from around the world.

Photograph by Allan Griffin

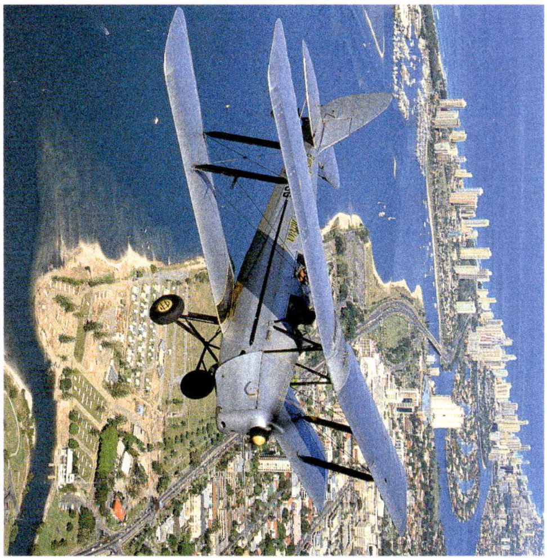

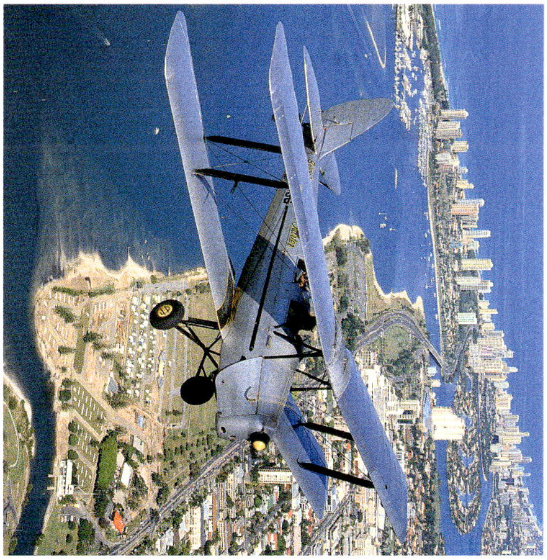

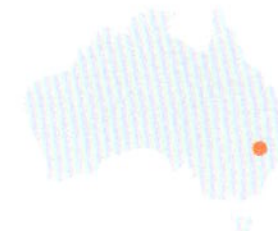

QUIRINDI RODEO, NSW

Australia's famous rodeos have always been a place for brave young men from the bush to test their skills. There is nothing like the whirling colours and distinctive sounds of a rodeo in full flight. To complete the atmosphere, a boisterous and knowledgeable crowd bedecked in large cowboy hats urges the riders on. This is the bull ride at Quirindi and beast seems to be getting the better of man in this particular chapter of the never-ending saga.

Similar stories are acted out at stockyards and country rodeos all around Australia because horses still play an important part in the Australian lifestyle and rural work.

The Australian bushman has always been a great rider, from the days of the famous Light Horse Brigade of Anzac fame, to *The Man From Snowy River* and *Clancy of the Overflow*. Even our most famous sporting institution, the Melbourne Cup, is based around the majesty of the horse.

Photograph by Allan Griffin

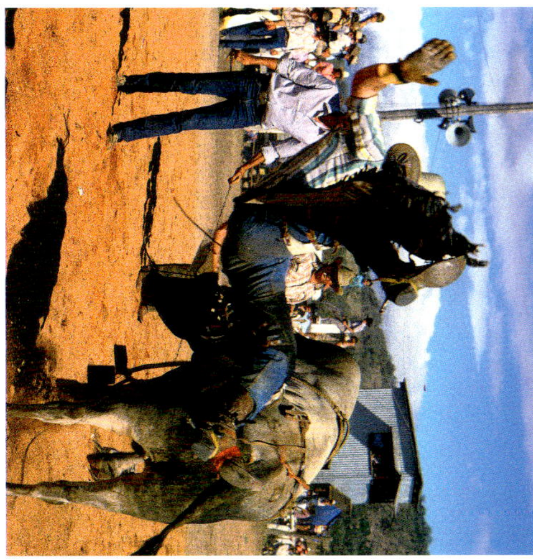

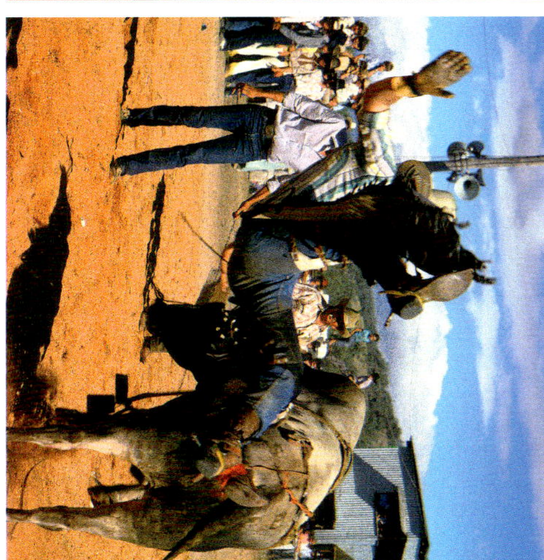

RED KANGAROO

The power and majesty of a red kangaroo in full flight is one of the great sights of outback Australia. The kings of the marsupial family, they are equally at home in harsh conditions or lush green pastures that accompany the coming of the inland rains. Marsupials produce their young at a very early stage of development and then suckle and protect them in their pouches for several months. This distinguishes them from all other mammals around the world.

Red kangaroos are the most widely distributed species of the 40 types in the kangaroo dynasty, being common throughout the dry inland areas of the continent. In the western areas both male and female are red, while in the east the male is red with a blue-grey head and tail and the female is totally blue, being known as a "blue flier".

Photograph by Leo Meier

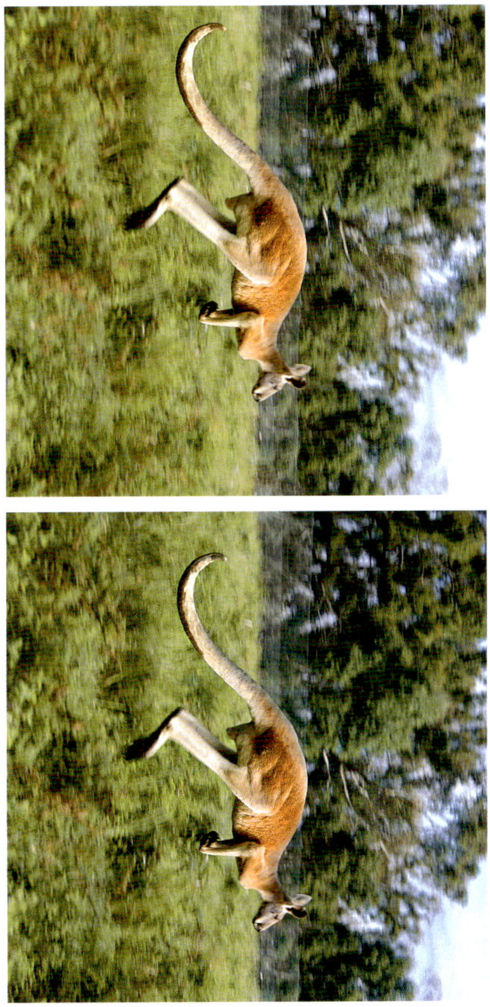

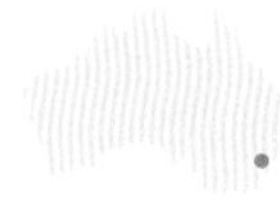

THREE SISTERS, KATOOMBA, NSW

One of Australia's most popular tourist attractions, The Three Sisters has drawn generations of visitors to gaze at the great beauty of the "ladies" and revel in the crisp, clean mountain air. Often crowded by tourists, the Echo Point viewing area features an interesting information centre as well as a healthy population of king parrots, galahs and crimson rosellas. There are plenty of well-marked walking trails available to escape the crowds and discover a secluded spot.

The Three Sisters is at the front doorstep of the tourist town it created – Katoomba. Here you will find cafés, guesthouses, luxury hotels and several attractions including the Skyway and the world's steepest passenger railway, the Scenic Railway, which was originally built to haul coal up the cliffs. Katoomba is within easy reach of Sydney, hence its popularity with international visitors, yet the surrounding Blue Mountains area is wild and hazardous. It is very easy to get lost in the blind canyons edged by sheer sandstone cliffs. Fierce bushfires and winter blizzards bear testimony to the harsh climate of the region, which appears gentle and benign at first appearance.

Photograph by David Stuckey

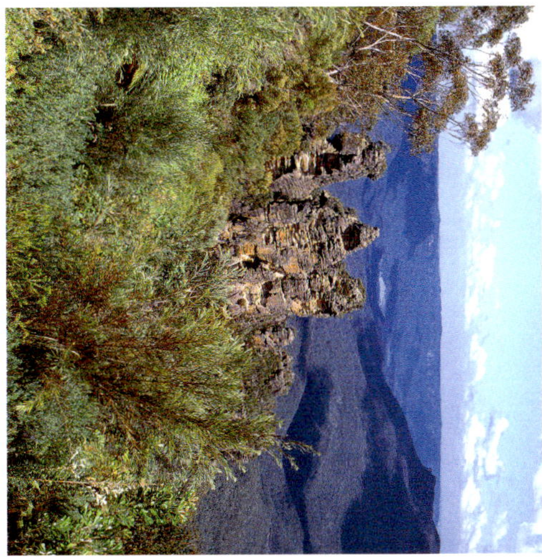

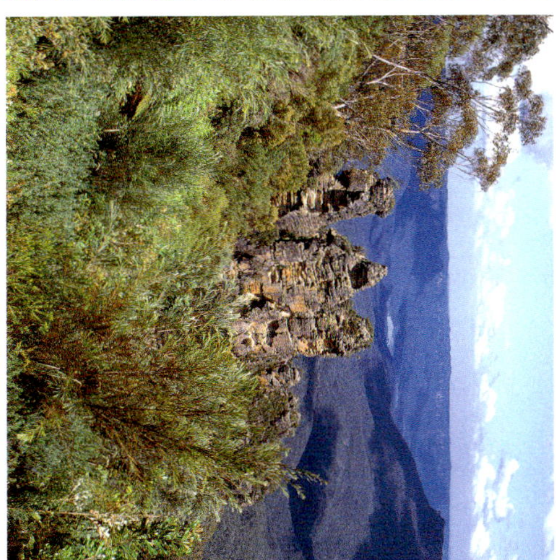

DESERT OAKS, ULURU, NT

It is said that when you stand beneath the desert oaks to the east of Uluru you can hear the earth breathe. It may just be the sound of the breeze in the slender leaves, but this is the true heart of Australia and it calls you back time and again. Although literally thousands of tourists gather to watch the spectacular sunset, sunrise at the rock is much quieter. It is a life-changing experience to sit in the cold desert air waiting for the first rays of dawn to appear. When the light strikes the rock, it sets the sandstone aglow with a red fiery light. The ever-changing light of the progressing sun transforms the rock throughout the day and it continually astounds with new shades of mauve, orange, red and purple. Uluru so dominates the landscape that you begin to see it as a living thing and you keep glancing at it to see what might happen next. This is Australia's heart, beating to an ancient rhythm that knows or cares nothing about the tribulations of modern man.

Photograph by Leo Meier

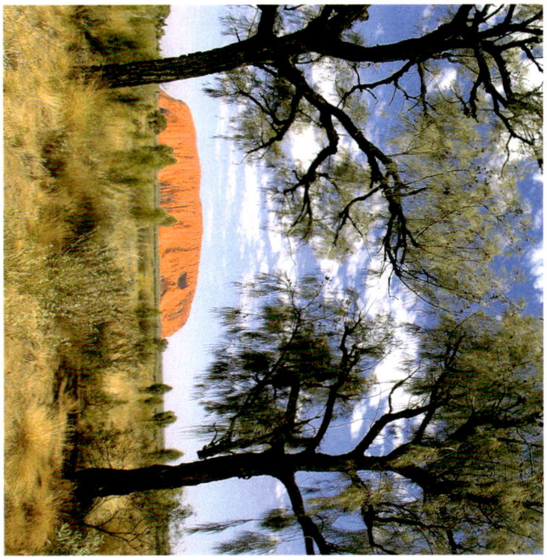

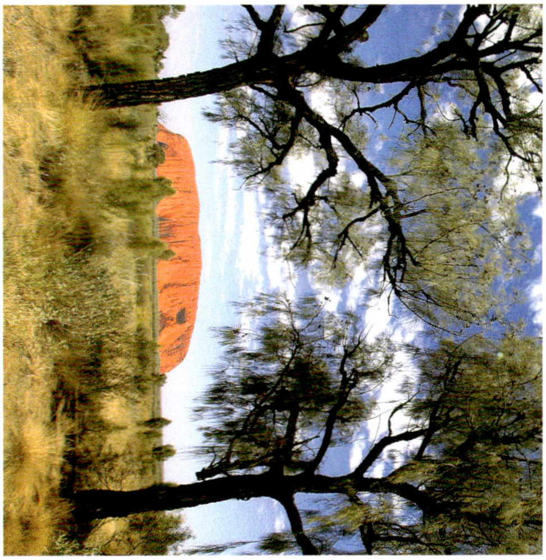

INDEX

KEN DUNCAN

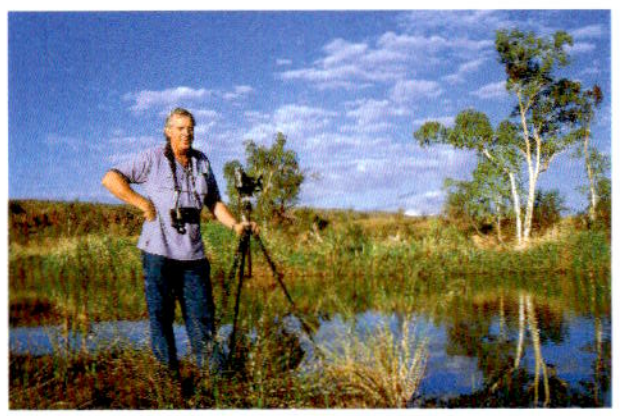

Ken Duncan, recognised internationally as a gifted and prolific landscape photographer with over 30 books to his credit, still chooses to describe himself as "...an average photographer with a great God". Ken is truly passionate about his craft, always striving for excellence, and travels extensively all over the world in search of the panoramic landscapes for which he is best known. Although Ken is well versed in a variety of photographic formats, this book is his first major foray into the wonderful world of 3-D. Undoubtedly it will not be his last.

www.kenduncan.com

LEO MEIER

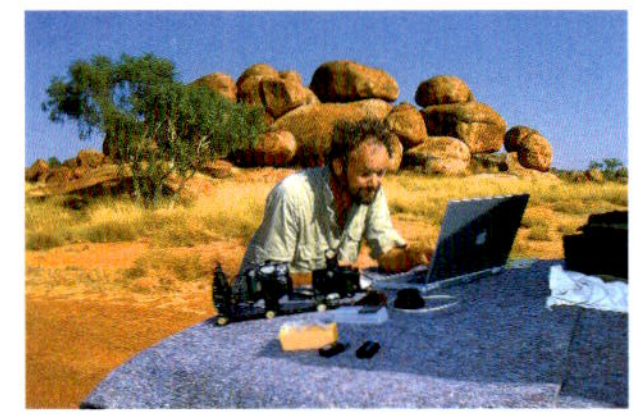

Leo Meier, recognised as one of Australia's leading photographers, has shot more than 20 books, many requiring epic journeys into some of the world's most remote regions. He has also been a contributor to 29 international books and many other high profile magazines. Leo's expertise spans 25 years and covers printing, graphic arts, photography, digital imaging and publishing. Leo has a genius for invention and over the years has designed and built a large array of unique equipment, including the specialised stereo camera rigs used in the photography for this book.

www.leomeier.com.au

3D AUSTRALIA
First published in 2003 by Ken Duncan Panographs® Pty Limited
ABN 21 050 235 606
PO Box 3015 Wamberal NSW 2260 Australia
Telephone +61 2 4367 6777
e-mail: panos@kenduncan.com

Designed by Open Art Surgery
Text by Dallas Sherringham
Edited by Pamela Duncan
Colour separations by Created for Life Pty Ltd
Front cover plate by David Burder and Performance Printing
Printed and bound in China

The National Library of Australia Cataloguing-in-Publication entry:
Duncan, Ken
3D Australia – An Awesome 3-Dimensional Experience
Includes index
ISBN 0 9580544 4 4
1. Australia – Pictorial works. I. Meier, Leo, 1951–. II. Title
919 400222

VISIT THE KEN DUNCAN GALLERY ONLINE
www.kenduncan.com